a pocketful of
RHYME
Imagination for a new generation

2006 Poetry Competition for 7-11 year-olds
YoungWriters

Poems From Surrey
Edited by Heather Killingray

 Young**Writers**

First published in Great Britain in 2007 by:
Young Writers
Remus House
Coltsfoot Drive
Peterborough
PE2 9JX
Telephone: 01733 890066
Website: www.youngwriters.co.uk

SB ISBN 978-1 84602 761 1

Foreword

Young Writers was established in 1991 and has been passionately devoted to the promotion of reading and writing in children and young adults ever since. The quest continues today. Young Writers remains as committed to the nurturing of poetic and literary talent as ever.

This year's Young Writers competition has proven as vibrant and dynamic as ever and we are delighted to present a showcase of the best poetry from across the UK and in some cases overseas. Each poem has been selected from a wealth of *A Pocketful Of Rhyme* entries before ultimately being published in this, our fourteenth primary school poetry series.

Once again, we have been supremely impressed by the overall quality of the entries we have received. The imagination, energy and creativity which has gone into each young writer's entry made choosing the poems a challenging and often difficult but ultimately hugely rewarding task - the general high standard of the work submitted ensured this opportunity to bring their poetry to a larger appreciative audience.

We sincerely hope you are pleased with this final collection and that you will enjoy *A Pocketful Of Rhyme Poems From Surrey* for many years to come.

Contents

Cuddington Community Primary School
Samuel Jackson (9)   1
James Youren (10)   1
Ayah El-obaidi (9)   2

Monks Orchard Primary School
Sam Bing (10)   2
Shannon Roper (8)   3
Marla Miller (10)   3
Dabiel Dodoo (9)   4
Victoria Robson (8)   4
Adrian Bascoe (10)   5
Michael Osei-Bonsu (9)   5
Chloe Hayes (7)   6
A J Moore (8)   6
Olivia Evans-Brown (7)   6
Roshan Grant (8)   7
Bobbi-Jay Deegan (8)   7
Cassius Crick (7)   7
Regina Osei-Bonsu (7)   8
Jack Reynolds (8)   8
Joshua Pooley (8)   8
Ethan Hazzard (8)   9
Shadhi Rowe (8)   9
Irene Goran (8)   9
Tempany Malcolm (8)   10
Amy Afriyie (8)   10
Reyon Dillon (8)   10
Megan Casban (8)   11
Oliver Savill (8)   11
Emily Kent (8)   11
Aghogho Agbinor (8)   12
Rebecca Garner (8)   12
Lauren Gallacher (7)   12
Caitlin Subit (8)   13
Ben Goss (7)   13
Roshani Kulendran (7)   13
Callum Crisp (8)   14
Alex Bird (7)   14

Lewis Bromley (7)	14
Bobby Earle (8)	15
T-Jay Harfleet-Diboll (7)	15
Kyle Crafton (7)	15
Moesha Rowe-Hinkson (9)	16
Jack Denman (7)	16
Kiera Borg (9)	17
Jennifer Lawson (7)	17
Leanne Villaverde (9)	18
Kane Lawe (11)	18
Toyanne Nelson-Thomas (10)	19
Danielle Semple (10)	19
Pamela Manful (7)	20
Harry Herbert (11)	20
Todd Fraser (7)	20
James Threadgill (9)	21
Lonica Palmer (9)	21
Daniel Louder (9)	21
Isabelle Evans-Brown (10)	22
Chloe Turner (10)	22
Jack Harman (11)	23
Dimitri Jeanneton (10)	23
George Williamson (10)	24
Nelson Jones -Stutter (10)	24
Rosie Peploe (10)	25
Symeera Allsop (10)	25
Kyle Andrews (10)	26
Lennox Antwi-Boasiako (10)	26
Jemma Smith (10)	27
Jack Woodward (10)	27
Debbie-Ann Ofosuware (11)	28
Antony Brady (10)	28
Aheesan Sivarasa (8)	29
Stephanie Ockwell (10)	29
Perri Palmer (10)	30
Ryan Freemantle (9)	30
Eunice Power (10)	31
Jodie Walker (9)	31
Kerri Steer (9)	32
Abigail Grimwood (8)	32
Rowan Bascoe (10)	33
Travis Jones (10)	33

Emily Algar (9)	34
Hollie Peploe (9)	34
Alex Clements (8)	34
Megan Delahunty (9)	35
Oliver Bennett (9)	35
Chloe Upfold (10)	35
Harry Riches (8)	36
Okenwa Okonkwo (8)	36
Olwyn O'Gorman (8)	36
Thomas Palmer (8)	37
Daniel Bowry (8)	37
Shannon Brooker (8)	37
Bethany Atkins-Mandell (8)	38
Elliott Evans (8)	38
Muhamed Taras (8)	38
Reshmi Ladwa (8)	39
Shannon Clarke-Marcelle (8)	39
Shannon Elliott (8)	39
Rhiannon Tole (9)	40
Alexander Stewart (10)	40
Roshan Roberts (10)	41
Joshua Lartey (11)	42
Laura McCarthy (10)	42
Daniel Harris (11)	43
Thomas Kallas (10)	43
Lauren Trout (11)	44
Jobi Freeman-Lampard (10)	45
Danielle Addison (11)	46
Anthony Young (10)	47
Atlanta Gunstone (10)	48
Taylor May (10)	48
Namirah Anderson (7)	49
Michael Greaves (7)	49
Chloe Scott (8)	49

St Catherine's Prep School, Guildford

Ellen Dickinson (9)	50

Seaton House School

Gabrielle Puleston-Vaudrey (7)	50
Onyeka Ambrose (9)	51

Olivia Keen (8)	51
Felicity Goldsack (9)	52
Emily Gibson (9)	52
Laura Hutchins (10)	53
Lucy Tarran (10)	54
Michelle Thompson (10)	55
Gemma Hutton (10)	56
Felicity O'Toole (10)	56
Annabelle Anyi Wang (10)	57

Thames Ditton Junior School

Georgina Howard (10)	57
Elizabeth Monaghan (8)	58
Giovanni Cornell-Lombardo (11)	59
Alice Ridsdale (8)	59
Erin Cummins (7)	60
David Cornell-Lombardo (9)	60
Georgia Imrie (10)	60
Georgina Pearson (7)	61
Hannah Phelps (8)	61
Kerry Alderson (10)	62
Heather Alderson (7)	62
Catherine Coxeter-Smith (7)	62
Sarah Macmillan (8)	63
Amy Horner (8)	63
Alice Harmer (7)	63
Morgan Burne (8)	64
Hannah Ridsdale (8)	64
Zoë Barr (9)	65
Natasha Thomas (8)	65

The Raleigh School

Emily Godwin (10)	66
Imogen Heenan (10)	66
Ellie Byrne (10)	67
Eleanor Wood (10)	67
Laura Douet (10)	67
Nicholas Allen (10)	68
Jemma Daniel (7)	68
Katy Nicholls (10)	69
Eve Hurcombe (10)	69

Megan Keepence (10)	70
Connor Paton (10)	70
Will Mead (9)	71
Freya Casserly (8)	71
Murray Hampshire (9)	72
Bradley Conisbee (9)	72
Scott Spencer (9)	73
Alexander Worsfold (9)	73
Rachel Butcher (9)	74
Phoebe Davies (10)	74
Gina Dyce (7)	75
Robert Peel (9)	75
Dominic Brown (9)	76
Emily Broome (9)	76
Ellie Punshon (9)	76
Clemmy Hill (10)	77
Daniel Steeden (10)	77
Chloe Holland (10)	78
Niall O'Hara (11)	78
Ellie Bonwick (7)	79
April Saunders (10)	79
Aaron Henderson (10)	80
Emily Clifford (10)	80
Mitchell Robinson (9)	81
Rebecca Witherspoon (10)	82
Matthew Mole (9)	82
Dillon Millington (9)	83
Emily Merry (9)	83
Monika Smith (9)	84
William Schaale (9)	84
Ellen Phillpot (9)	85
Jonathan Finch (9)	85
India Davies (9)	86
Melissa Williams (9)	86
Andrew Wells (9)	87
Katie Tame (9)	87
Jade Warr (8)	88
Harry Bennett (9)	88
Ellie Judd (10)	89
Oliver Hassard (9)	89
Hannah Hill (10)	90
Victoria Holloway (10)	90

Oliver Hind (9)		91
Emily Runton (10)		91
Charlotte Piears (10)		92
Samuel Gilbert (10)		93
Ellie Whitlock (10)		94
Callum Nixon (10)		94
Holly Stroud (10)		95
Olivia Ellis (10)		95
Christie Dowling (10)		96
Matt Gould (10)		96
Eleanor Johnston (10)		97
Ellie Feary (8)		97
Isobel Marsh (7)		98
Jessica Caulder (9)		98
Claire Robinson (9)		99
Jessica De Carvalho (9)		99
Verity Barnes (11)		100
Alice Thacker (8)		101
Ben Lock (10)		102
William Stanford (9)		102
Christopher Bennett (8)		103
Millie Franks (9)		103
Dominic Rawlins (8)		104
Stuart McCully (8)		104
Joseph Nicholson (9)		105
Emma Tallick (10)		105
Megan Richards (7)		106
Imogen Harms (7)		106
Kay Bainbridge (7)		107
Marcus Hutchings (7)		107
Eleanor Chard (9)		108
Angus Cook (9)		108
Edward Barber (9)		109
Alice Richardson (9)		109
Ben Thompson (10)		110
Oliver Harry (10)		110
Joshua Henderson (7)		111
Katie Thacker (9)		111
Oliver Beney (10)		112
James Smith (10)		112
Rebecca Fox (10)		113

The Poems

Football

On Monday afternoon we play football in the park
We like to kick-off early before it gets dark

We have to choose our sides and choose them really quick
But the boy always left to last, is poor Rick

His shorts are too long and his boots don't fit
So that's why even his friends take the mick

I'm best as a defender and that's my usual role
If I get to play up front then I try to score a goal

We race from one end to the other, fighting for the ball
We have to stop their attack so we use the off-side rule

When I get home all muddy having scored the only goal
Mum sends me off to wash my hands in the bowl

My team we are the best and we win all our games
I'm going to have my picture taken and Mum will put it in a frame.

Samuel Jackson (9)
Cuddington Community Primary School

Sunflower

The sunflower is like the sun in the sky and a fireball flying
                                                    through the air
It is the golden light from a lantern and brings happiness to all
Each little petal is like a miniature bar of gold
It grows as high as the sky, resting steady on a thin, but strong stem
When you look at it, it will bring imaginary warmth to those who are cold
It is like a tiny, round, brown planet shrouded in flame.

James Youren (10)
Cuddington Community Primary School

Frlends!

F for having fun with all your best mates
R for having races to the school gates
I for intelligence when you lend
E for eating lunch with your friend
N for being nice and helpful
D for determination to be *cool*
S for saying thanks to the school because we have
  such good friends!
  But it still means that my friends are the best.

Ayah El-obaidi (9)
Cuddington Community Primary School

The Blitz

Wailing sirens break the dead of night
Disastrous danger
Bombs dropping
Devastation across the nation
Reflection of fierce burning fires in innocent people's eyes
Smoky flames burst into houses tearing them to mountains of rubble
Choking fumes seep into the musty shelter
Distant shrieks, all hope has vanished
I wrap a damp old cloth around my ears
To stop the deafening sound echoing through my mind
I fall asleep, eyes filled with tears
Yet I hear the drone of planes overhead
The Germans salute as Englishmen die.

Sam Bing (10)
Monks Orchard Primary School

The Orange

The orange is round and it is orange and it smells fantastic
The orange is more beautiful than a pumpkin
The orange is juicy and when you eat it, it makes your face squelch
because it's sour
The orange is a yummy piece of fruit and it is delicious
The orange is big and when you cut it open, inside there's lots of seeds
in the orange
The orange is shaped like a circle and it is very weird.

Shannon Roper (8)
Monks Orchard Primary School

The Blitz

Sirens wailing
While the Germans bomb our country
The mother tries to comfort the child, saying it's only thunder
Someone's coughing and choking
Lightning strikes down, high speed
I smell smoke, it smells awful
I feel angry and outside is all misty
I feel tried and weary, anxious and afraid
Outside the blackness hides the rubble
Destruction is everywhere.

Marla Miller (10)
Monks Orchard Primary School

The Apple

The apple is as soft as a smooth banana
The apple is hard and crunchy
The apple is sometimes red and green
The apple is very squashy and also sour
The apple is bumpy, squishy and so juicy
The apple is crunchy and very green
The apple is very delicious and tasty
The apple is as hard as metal
The apple is as crunchy as a carrot
The apple is as big as an orange.

Dabiel Dodoo (9)
Monks Orchard Primary School

Solar System

S tars, stars, lots of stars
O nly a few planets
L ike Earth, Mars and Saturn
A round the sun they go
R evolving and turning all the time

S un, satellites and spaceships
Y ou probably have seen it in a book
S howing pictures of planets
T he *biggest* planet is Jupiter
E arth is next to Mars
M ars is a very hot planet.

Victoria Robson (8)
Monks Orchard Primary School

Young Writers - A Pocketful Of Rhyme Poems From Surrey

The Blitz

In 1940 I laid in my cosy bed
Then I heard a monstrous bang
So I jumped out of my luxurious bed
While I got out of the house this is what I saw:
Demolition all over
Fear in petrified eyes
As bombs dropped a devastating blizzard
Frowns on lonely faces
More nervous than ever
It was too late for evacuation
Lives going by the second
However Hitler's just doing his job
Swearing like crazy or you could say berserk
The town is like a dartboard
All becoming weaker
Losing all sense of hope
As German planes whizz by.

Adrian Bascoe (10)
Monks Orchard Primary School

Strawberry

The strawberry is as red-hot as lava
The strawberry is as red as blood
The strawberry is as red as lipstick
The strawberry is as red as an apple
The strawberry is so tasty and sweet.

Michael Osei-Bonsu (9)
Monks Orchard Primary School

Strawberries

S trawberries are red and heart-shaped
T hey are scrummy to eat
R ipe strawberries are as red as a ruby
A re my favourite fruit
W ow, how tasty
B etter for you than a sugary chocolate bar
E very day I eat one because they are so delicious
R ed and lovely to eat
R efreshing in a smoothie with a banana
Y ummy in my tummy.

Chloe Hayes (7)
Monks Orchard Primary School

Apple

An apple is juicy like a strawberry
An apple is like a kiwi
An apple is tastier than a banana
An apple is heavier than sweetcorn
An apple is squishier than a banana
An apple is shiny, bright red, more than a pumpkin
An apple is shiny and gold
An apple is pure red like a strawberry.

A J Moore (8)
Monks Orchard Primary School

Apples

A pples are crunchy and nice to eat
P recious and delicious fruit to me
P ears just cannot compete
L ovely and juicy fruit always
E xquisite apples are very sweet.

Olivia Evans-Brown (7)
Monks Orchard Primary School

Young Writers - A Pocketful Of Rhyme Poems From Surrey

The Pineapple

The pineapple is a short tree with spikes
The pineapple is a tree stump cut off
The pineapple is an enormous egg with a bitter taste
The pineapple is a yellow throne for Miss Garner
The pineapple will fill your mouth with a spectacular taste
The pineapple will blow you away when you eat it
The pineapple is a giant waiting for its prey to eat it
The pineapple is a small yellow car
The pineapple is a wrestler's ring
The pineapple is as sticky as honey.

Roshan Grant (8)
Monks Orchard Primary School

The Apple

The apple is as red as a juicy tomato
The apple is an acrobatic apple
The apple has a really tall stalk
The apple is as red as a cherry, it's an acidic and spotty apple
The apples have been grown, washed and taken to shops and stalls
The apples are sweet and squashy
I love apples!

Bobbi-Jay Deegan (8)
Monks Orchard Primary School

Dogs I Love

D ogs are cute and cuddly
O ff they go running around
G etting all muddy
S un shining on their fur coats.

Cassius Crick (7)
Monks Orchard Primary School

Strawberries

S weet and looks like red ice in the middle
T asty, really sweet and looks like red icing in the middle
R ed spotty strawberries, delicious to eat
A lways tasty, smells really sweet
W onderful strawberries, never takes long to ripen
B ig strawberries, always delicious to eat
E qual strawberries, gazing in the sun
R ipened strawberries, tasty to eat
R eally sweet, like sweet toffee
Y ucky sometimes when I've had too many.

Regina Osei-Bonsu (7)
Monks Orchard Primary School

The Banana

The banana is as yellow as a shiny sparkler
The banana is smooth and is really yummy
The banana is quite yummy and is soft and easy to eat
The banana is as sweet as a cup of tea
The banana wears a smooth coat of yellow
The banana is a big bendy banana like a boomerang.

Jack Reynolds (8)
Monks Orchard Primary School

Sweetcorn

The sweetcorn is a very bumpy vegetable
The sweetcorn looks like a tooth
The sweetcorn is put together tidily
The sweetcorn is a satisfying vegetable
The sweetcorn is so sweet.

Joshua Pooley (8)
Monks Orchard Primary School

The Cherry

A cherry is as red as the reddest traffic light
A cherry is as bright as the red-hot sun
A cherry can brighten up your day
A cherry is as juicy as a bright orange
A cherry is as tiny as a small ant
A cherry is as soft as a red strawberry
A cherry is so bright it can blind your eyes.

Ethan Hazzard (8)
Monks Orchard Primary School

The Carrot

The carrot smells like orange juicy but slimy
The carrot is underground
The carrot is very sweet
The carrot is from Africa
The carrot can be cut
The carrot is spiky
The carrot is spiky as a dead grass
The carrot is nasty as a peanut.

Shadhi Rowe (8)
Monks Orchard Primary School

Red Cherries

The cherry is as red as a rose
The cherry is red, soft and sweet
They normally grow on trees
They have red juice, tasty and sour
The cherries are as chewy as chewing gum
The cherries are as red as red wine
Cherries have a smell more beautiful than posh perfume.

Irene Goran (8)
Monks Orchard Primary School

Passion Fruit

The passion fruit is like an orange but with black seeds in the middle
The passion fruit is as prickly as a perky pineapple
The passion fruit is as wet and slippery as icy white snow
The passion fruit grows in hot countries only
The passion fruit is as red and as scrumptious as strawberries
The passion fruit is as delicious as red strawberries
The passion fruit is as edible as brown chocolate.

Tempany Malcolm (8)
Monks Orchard Primary School

The Stupendous Strawberry

The strawberries come from the ground
The sensible sweet strawberries, stupendous strawberries
The strawberries are sweet and a bit rough
The strawberries taste like a lollipop in my mouth
The strawberries smell really sweet
The strawberries look like a red nose
The inside of the strawberries look like red ice.

Amy Afriyie (8)
Monks Orchard Primary School

The Carrot

The carrot is orange as a goldfish
The carrot is small and fat
The carrot is clean, rough and fresh
The carrot is crispy like cornflakes
The carrot is like a pencil
The carrot is scaly.

Reyon Dillon (8)
Monks Orchard Primary School

The Parsnip

The parsnip is made of clear white water like crunchy snow
The parsnip is as soft as a piece of sleepy snow
The parsnip is as tiny as a zippy, powerful zebra
The parsnip is as dirty as a dusty, muddy greyhound, *woof, woof!*
The parsnip is as rough on the front as a rottweiler (that's very rough!)
The parsnip is as edible as chocolate, when it is dirty it is as brown
                                                            as chocolate
The parsnip is as crispy as an orange, edible, scrumptious carrot.

Megan Casban (8)
Monks Orchard Primary School

The Apple

An apple is a sun painted green and red
An apple is a ball painted green and red and pushed in at the top
An apple is a brick, shaped like a round ball
An apple is an edible cannonball
An apple is as red as hot lava
An apple is as green as silky grass.

Oliver Savill (8)
Monks Orchard Primary School

The Banana

The banana is cold like the North Pole
The banana is as thick as snow
The banana is a yellow sun
The banana is as light as a feather
The banana is as bright as a light bulb
The banana is a yellow flower.

Emily Kent (8)
Monks Orchard Primary School

The Apple

The apple is as red as a rose in the moonlight sky, sparkling
The apple is delicious as a chocolate but a healthy version
The apple tastes like a fruitful piece of orange
The apple is an amazing powerful apple and it is so good
I can't take my mouth off it
The apple is an apricoty apple and it just doesn't run out of taste
The apple is an astonished apple and it is like fruit salad
The apple is a wonderful apple and it is fabulous, full of life.

Aghogho Agbinor (8)
Monks Orchard Primary School

The Banana

The banana is a big bendy banana
The banana is golden and yellow like the sun
The banana is as yellow as a sun
The banana is as golden as a golden bird
The banana is soft as a teddy bear
The banana is difficult to peel.

Rebecca Garner (8)
Monks Orchard Primary School

Cats

C ats can be funny
A nd leap around the house
T ake your cat indoors when it gets cold outside
S o that your cat won't catch a cold.

Lauren Gallacher (7)
Monks Orchard Primary School

The Strawberry

The strawberry is as satisfying as sweetcorn
The strawberry's seeds are like specks of dust
The strawberry is a curved triangle fitted with tiny seeds
The strawberry is a pool filled with sweetness
The strawberry is made from precious flowers that emerge
                                         from underground.

Caitlin Subit (8)
Monks Orchard Primary School

Football

F ancy footwork on the pitch
O thers tackling for the ball
O n my team we have the best
T rying to score a wicked goal
B all coming to my feet
A bout to score a goal
L aughing and cheering all around
L uckily I've scored, we have won!

Ben Goss (7)
Monks Orchard Primary School

Owls

O wls hoot in the dark night
W hen owls sleep we wake up
L ooking for lovely food to eat
S leepy when the sun gets up.

Roshani Kulendran (7)
Monks Orchard Primary School

Football

F ootball is my favourite sport
O h my, yes it is
O h lots of trophies for football I have
T here flies the ball into the goal
B reaking the net as it goes in
A ll the time we beat a team
L eader of the scoreboard
L loyd Park is where we play

T he wicked Wickham Wanderers are who I play for
E very team we have beaten
A t least exactly
M any teams aren't as good as us.

Callum Crisp (8)
Monks Orchard Primary School

Animals

A nimals come in all shapes and sizes
N ice ones and nasty ones
I like the fast bouncy kangaroo
M y favourites are furry and cute
A nimals can be friendly or fierce
L ots can be kept as pets
S mall or large, I love them all.

Alex Bird (7)
Monks Orchard Primary School

Wolf

W olves they hang around in packs
O nly nice to family and friends
L istening carefully for their prey
F inishing the night with a howl.

Lewis Bromley (7)
Monks Orchard Primary School

Flower Pot

F eed flowers in the pot
L ying in the sun
O n dirty dirt
W inning a competition to buy more seed
E lephants eat my seed
R eally good flowers rising in the sun

P ictures of lovely flowers in the different lands
O h no, the elephants took my seeds again
T ime's up! Three flowers left that's how good the sun has been
   giving the flowers a chance to grow.

Bobby Earle (8)
Monks Orchard Primary School

School

S chool is fun
C ome and play
H omework is boring
O nly from Monday to Friday
O ther children play with me
L earning is excellent.

T-Jay Harfleet-Diboll (7)
Monks Orchard Primary School

Stars

S tars light up the sky at night
T hey twinkle in the dark sky
A nd make it shine so bright
R emember to wish when you see
S hooting stars make a wish for me.

Kyle Crafton (7)
Monks Orchard Primary School

Incredible Africans!

Bright yellow and burnt orange fabric
Swishing and swaying swiftly like
The golden gleaming sun

Skilful hands tapping on the brown, bulky, big base drum
Trained dancers prancing and prancing
Tap! Tap! Tap! says the drum
Spotted hyenas fill the air
As children laugh, clap and stare

Bang! Bang! Bang! of the stamping feet
Everyone is lively and dancing to the frantic beat

Exhausted, panting, breathless as the drum beats
The ground starts to shake
The distant drums start to beat
Rainforest leaves rustle and shake
Dust flows around like a dusty tornado.

Moesha Rowe-Hinkson (9)
Monks Orchard Primary School

Sport

S nooker is a very calm sport
P utting is a very slow bit of golf
O n the pitch I play football
R un on the pitch with my team mates
T aking part in other sports is fun.

Jack Denman (7)
Monks Orchard Primary School

Danzefuzion Diva

At Danzefuzion you can see
People moving as can be
When you move left to right
You seem to look like a great big kite.

At Danzefuzion you can hear
Lots of people having a cheer
Danzefuzion is the best
We love to dance
We will impress
It keeps us fit
And smiling too
So we are here to entertain you.

Danzefuzion makes you feel
Like going up a steep hill
And dancing till the break of dawn
Then dancing on your front lawn.

Kiera Borg (9)
Monks Orchard Primary School

Friends

F riends are great to play with
R unning about and having fun
I think my friends are lovely
E veryone has a brilliant time
N ever will you be lonely
D on't ever think they won't play with you
S pecial to me all the time.

Jennifer Lawson (7)
Monks Orchard Primary School

Dancing In The African Village

Colours so bright makes my eyes open wide
Drums so brown like the bark of an ancient tree
Drum skin circular and smooth like the glittery drifting moon
Boom! Boom! Boom! went their feet as they skimmed
the rock-hard floor
'Ha! Ha!' screamed the children as they ran around the ball
like huge hungry lions
As scared as a fly stuck in a shiny sparkly web
Bursting with happiness like a volcano about to explode.

Leanne Villaverde (9)
Monks Orchard Primary School

Evacuation

As I stand at the platform, dull and bare
My bag hanging off my weak, bruised back
I wait in a line waiting to get a tag
Tied on my tatty braces
I burst into tears, it's too late to say goodbye again
My mum's face fading in the distance
As the train leaves the platform.

As I sit on the train thinking
What my carer will be like
I stare out the window
Seeing fields, farms and that makes me wonder
Will I be sleeping in a shed tonight or in a comfy room?
I wonder if I will be getting what I want.

Kane Lawe (11)
Monks Orchard Primary School

Dancing In The School

Orange and yellow fabric like the afternoon sky when the sun sets
Terracotta tambourine being tapped on with skilful hands,
Professional dancers prancing
Like a sailing ship on the angry and roaring sea, children laughing
Like the sun gleaming in the light blue heavens

Frantic beat, tapping feet, laughing as the dance repeats
The room fills with heat
As there's loads of constant tapping feet to the delirious beat
Not even keeping up with the time
Feeling energetic, feeling fine
Ever so cheerful through the hour
Feeling like I get the power.

Toyanne Nelson-Thomas (10)
Monks Orchard Primary School

The Blitz

Sleeping peacefully in my bed
Vibrations under my head
I feel petrified
Quickly, quietly run to the shelter
I smell the damp
It's making me feel cold
Peeping through the hole to see demolished houses
See the terror in people's eyes

Check to make sure your house is still standing
A silence fills the street, you could only hear
The miaows from a terrified cat
Broken by the all-clear
At last.

Danielle Semple (10)
Monks Orchard Primary School

Outside

G rass swaying in the breeze
A nd be careful, don't graze my knee
R ound and round I go on a tree
D amp and dirty I can even see a bee
E veryone says it is dusty as me
N o, no, no, that is not right, get some money or I'll give you a fright.

Pamela Manful (7)
Monks Orchard Primary School

The Blitz

Sirens blaring like a thousand cats screaming
Fires burning fiercely
Screams and cries fill our ears
As we race to the shelter
The vibration of the bombs
Makes my legs buckle
Suddenly silence
As the last plane flies back
A job well done
As Hitler toasts to the job in hand.

Harry Herbert (11)
Monks Orchard Primary School

Healthy

H ave a delicious pomegranate
E ating it is fun
A ll those lovely seeds
L ots of goodness just for me
T eeth are munching and crunching
H aving fruit is good
Y ummy in my tummy.

Todd Fraser (7)
Monks Orchard Primary School

Harvest Festival

Farmers working as hard as they can, growing fresh food for everyone
Crunchy, golden-brown leaves falling from trees that blow gently
in the wind
The sweetness of the ripened fruits can satisfy any hunger, quench
any thirst
Touching the food grown by the farmers, I remember all the things
God has given us.

James Threadgill (9)
Monks Orchard Primary School

Harvest Festival

The golden-brown leaves slowly swirling to the dusty ground
Leaves being tossed into the air like an aeroplane taking off
In the morning I touch the warm crispy bread on my white shiny plate
I feel like I can make a difference and I feel sad for all the people
in the world
Who have no home and need our help
Harvest is for helping!

Lonica Palmer (9)
Monks Orchard Primary School

Harvest Festival

The people gathering their wonderful crop in their golden fields
The golden-brown leaves blowing across the smooth autumn floor
A sweet, bright, red apple fresh from the bushy tree
The rough surface of an old purple turnip
I feel thankful for all the things we receive.

Daniel Louder (9)
Monks Orchard Primary School

The Blitz

Children breaking the silence, crying
Concerned parents calling, 'Help!'
Blazing fires leaving colossal destruction
Engines roaring loudly above me
Demolished houses all around
Rubble everywhere on the ground
People are looking at the burning fires
Feeling so mournful and extremely tired
Calm parents are trying to say,
'Children, children, there's no need to be afraid.'
But still they run from the dreadful sights
Racing frantically, trying to hide
Our world is being contaminated, there's pollution in the air
But Hitler just doesn't seem to care.

Isabelle Evans-Brown (10)
Monks Orchard Primary School

The Blitz

A siren startles me
Shivers gallop through my body
My mum pulls me to the bomb shelter
And holds me tightly in her trembling arms
We hear bombs roaring to the ground
Then deadly silence
Shattered windows, bricks and rubble
A lost city
We stand, we stare, slowly the sound comes to us
A groaning body in the mud.

Chloe Turner (10)
Monks Orchard Primary School

The Blitz

In bed sleeping like the dead
Suddenly I was awoken by a siren
Howling through the air
I hurried to the shelter and rested there
During the night I felt the vibrations
I heard the whistling of the bombs dropping
Next morning there were blazing fires everywhere
Bombs in every place you could see
I turned to go into my house, but there was only rubble
I couldn't help but shed tears, I was devastated
There were so many bodies, if it were not for the shelter
One of them could have been me
But where was Mum?
I looked around and saw her there on the floor
Was she dead or alive?
I checked, but she was gone
I sobbed my eyes out
I couldn't accept that Mum was gone.

Jack Harman (11)
Monks Orchard Primary School

The Blitz

The German planes keep whizzing by
Dropping bombs, the people would die
The sounds of the sirens will make babies cry
The smoke of planes is killing me
Bits of rubble hitting me
The Germans are getting closer
The wind is getting slower
I feel my blood getting colder
Hitler's getting bolder and older.

Dimitri Jeanneton (10)
Monks Orchard Primary School

The Blitz

Babies, whining, people dying
Bombs falling, wardens talking
Germans flying, England's crying
Shelters crowded, toddlers surrounded
Pilots fighting as fast as lightning
Doodlebugs whistling, citizens hoping
Homes destroyed, everyone annoyed
Broken windows, too many widowed
So much violence in the silence
Laying sleepless, rest the RAF
Waiting for tomorrow, so much sorrow
Planes soaring, England's lions roaring.

George Williamson (10)
Monks Orchard Primary School

The Blitz

As planes fly, England cries
Bombs meet their destination
Blowing up half the nation
Bombs screaming
Children fleeing
Nurses helping
Wounded patients
As I cry, people die
Mother says, 'Please keep calm.'
But sweat pours out of me
Inside the shelter, I wait silently.

Nelson Jones -Stutter (10)
Monks Orchard Primary School

The Blitz

Children break the silence by crying
Anxious parents scream for help
Blazing fires leave destruction
Engines roar above us
From the planes in the sky
Ruined houses all around
Rubble everywhere
People stare at the fires
Devastated and tired
Vibrations in the Anderson shelter
Damp smells making it worse
Outside shrieking, crying
Calm parents trying to say,
'Children, children, there is no need to be afraid.'
Hot and bothered fire guards
Running frantically, trying to hide
Nothing left of our quiet little street.

Rosie Peploe (10)
Monks Orchard Primary School

The Blitz

Deafening explosions everywhere
Sirens screaming over there
Bombs dropping - people beware
Squabbling children filled with fear
Terrified parents holding them near
Trying so hard to hold back a tear
Smoky fumes surrounding the air
Hitler and his troops just don't care
Fear and devastation everywhere.

Symeera Allsop (10)
Monks Orchard Primary School

The Blitz

Wailing sirens break the dead of night
Diabolical danger
Bombs dropping
Devastation across the nation
Reflection of fire in innocent people's eyes
Smoky flames fly into the shelter
Be quick to get your mask on
Shelter gone, nowhere to go
Distant shrieks, all hope gone
Under a table I hear the bombs
I try to sleep but yet awaken
All the silence broken
I wrap cloth around my ears
I cry myself to sleep
When I wake up
The bombs have stopped
I am safe, but where's my family?

Kyle Andrews (10)
Monks Orchard Primary School

Evacuation

The sound of children saying goodbye
When I look out the window all I do is cry
My mum is not there she is in the house
I am five and I feel like a mouse
The sour city is leaving me
Hour by hour I see the country
The billeting officer takes me to my billet
She is nice, but her cat is insulting.

Lennox Antwi-Boasiako (10)
Monks Orchard Primary School

The Blitz

Hearing booming sirens once again
I rush rapidly outside in the pouring rain
In the shelter it's bitter and damp
I want to get out but it won't be safe
We're all like animals stuck in our enclosure
But suddenly we hear an almighty explosion
We wait a minute and then go out
I can't hear anything for a bit
Until a baby breaks the silence, with its crying
I stare in horror as I see the ruins of my old house
There's fire all around me
I burst into tears as I stumble over to the ruins
And find my old teddy on the floor
I scurry back to my parents, holding my teddy tight
Managing to get to the shelter, I sleep the rest of the night.

Jemma Smith (10)
Monks Orchard Primary School

The Blitz

Babies whining, people dying
Bombs dropping, wardens quietly talking
Germans flying, England's crying
Shelters crowded, toddlers surrounded
Rain falling, engines roaring
Suddenly silence
People dare to venture outside
Families find their beloved houses destroyed
All that remains is a lone brick.

Jack Woodward (10)
Monks Orchard Primary School

The Blitz

Fire blazing violently outside
The shelter's getting wet
The babies whining
Their mum says, 'Don't fret.'
Engines roaring
People quarrelling to get underground first
In the darkness, you can't see the planes soaring
You can see the weariness in victims' eyes
But anxious citizens, becoming nauseous, quivering with fear
Feeling the tension rise
As I count the unending hours, the distant cries of the ill-fated
I am furious, vexed
As our country is being bombed by the hate
Suddenly, dead silence
Waiting expectantly hoping
Desiring the war to be over
Praying diligently to end this violence
The warden's assuring us we're out of danger
I tiptoe out of the shelter, noticing mourning souls
I pity those poor strangers
Stepping barefoot on the icy ground
Standing on the rubble called my house
I weep despairingly without sound.

Debbie-Ann Ofosuware (11)
Monks Orchard Primary School

Harvest Festival

People are celebrating, thankful for the harvest food they've gathered
Farmers digging through the thick, dark mud to gather in sweet,
pale, golden potatoes
I am delighted, happy and eager to share this lovely food
with those who need it most
The poor, the old and the homeless
Farmers bringing in foods that give us sensations of flavour
A true taste of harvest.

Antony Brady (10)
Monks Orchard Primary School

Five Ways Of Looking At An Apple

The apple is a red rain dropping from the sky
The apple is like a ball getting kicked round the floor
The apple is juicy and delicious and it smells like a water melon
And is as tasty as anything
The apple is a ball and as shiny as the sun
The apple is so nice that I want one now.

Aheesan Sivarasa (8)
Monks Orchard Primary School

Evacuation!

Suddenly I am all alone
Cries and shouts all around
Like being wrapped in a cone
The train leaves its ground.

My idiot brother somewhere
Tall, dark strangers here and there
While the green, green grass passes by
And the flowers wave goodbye.

As I reach my destination
The billeting officer awaits me to come
My bag so itchy and my gas mask so heavy
Will my billet have some rum?

I finally meet my new billet
She doesn't look at all nice
Her name is Jillet
And she has pet mice.

Stephanie Ockwell (10)
Monks Orchard Primary School

The Blitz

An alarming siren startles me
Feeling shivers running wildly through my body
Mum tugs me speedily to the bomb shelter
Firmly grasping me in her shaking arms
We can hear speeding engines
Bombs roaring to the ground
Deadly silence all around
Shattered windows, rubble on the ground
A lost city to be found
We stop
We stare
What's that sound?
A howling body on the ground
Sobbing people flooding the streets with tears
Filled with dread and unthinkable fears
No home to go to, no tasty food to eat
All we can do is sit and weep
Hoping it will all be over
No bombs, crying or people dying.

Perri Palmer (10)
Monks Orchard Primary School

Harvest Festival

Cherries shining, glowing
Ecstatic people dancing.

A big cheer echoing
Through the silent city
As the harvest finishes.

Rusty leaves slowly swirl to the ground
As rushing people step and crush them.

Ryan Freemantle (9)
Monks Orchard Primary School

Evacuation

Looking out the train window, listening to the noise
Parents saying goodbye to all their boys
I was next to no one, just an empty seat
It seemed like the floor was miles from my feet
Sitting there just wondering who I'd meet
Or what I would say
All my friends were going far, far away
Clutted cotton clouds drifting through the sky
Questioning myself who, when and why?

The sun approaching my cheeks as leaving the train
Slowly then suddenly it begins to rain
Putting on my wellingtons, buttoning my coat
The thought of Mum leaves a lump in my throat
Queuing up for a gas mask, I hadn't already got
Mum isn't organised and she worries a lot.

Meeting my new billet, who is selfish and likes to be unseen
Being rude to the billeting officer who is dirty and unclean
Finally we get there to the new house
The bedrooms are so big, I feel like a mouse
There is so much luxury, but it isn't really home
Going to the stairs and sitting all alone.

Eunice Power (10)
Monks Orchard Primary School

Harvest Festival

Rustling leaves swirling onto the muddy ground
Orange, brown and yellow.

Crunchy, crispy, flat leaves like worn out carpet
Smooth, juicy, soft, tangy berries
Rough skin, prickly pineapples and soft bananas.

Feeling happy that autumn is here again.

Jodie Walker (9)
Monks Orchard Primary School

Harvest Festival

Brown, crunchy leaves dropping from the firm trees
Now autumn is here.

Joyful, loud children are playing in the fields
Because our glimmering yellow sun is out.

Soft, succulent corn tasting better and better in the air
Yippee! Harvest is here.

Hard, brown, circular conkers sitting on the stony ground
Because it's conker time!

I feel overjoyed and excited now,
Everyone is here!

Kerri Steer (9)
Monks Orchard Primary School

Six Ways Of Looking At A Banana

The banana is soft and sweet and has seeds inside
The banana grows on a tree in a hot country
The banana is as hard as a wrestler's chest
The banana is as smooth as a laminated piece of card
The banana is yummy and is a little bit bumpy
The banana is as bendy as the moon in the dark night.

Abigail Grimwood (8)
Monks Orchard Primary School

Evacuation

I hear the train rattle like bells
But I'm shaking like an earthquake
As I get on the steamy strain I sit with a stranger
However, my heart races harder and harder
But I think I'm in danger.

I am on my journey
I feel like I am left out
I even think that the billet will hate me.

Rowan Bascoe (10)
Monks Orchard Primary School

Evacuation

My mum was crying to the kids, 'Off you go.'
The whistle blew
The train left
Off we went to the country
The mothers were crying to their children
We were in the countryside
The train arrived at the station
The billet officer came down from the steep, steep hill
Soon I would know where I was going.

Travis Jones (10)
Monks Orchard Primary School

Harvest Festival

Golden corn in the brown field swaying in the wind
Like a ballerina dancing to classical music.

Leaves are crackling on the frost ground
Like a chop of an apple.

Sweet cherries like a big balloon popping
When you taste the sweetness.

Winter is coming, soon this beauty will be frozen
I feel happy now, people have food.

Emily Algar (9)
Monks Orchard Primary School

Harvest Festival

People celebrating as they bring their fresh vegetables into school
Dirty tractors trudging through the narrow lanes between
the golden fields
The sweetness of the red rose apples make my mouth water
As I ate the ripe red apple, I felt the sweetness run down my throat
When I touch the crunchy leaves they went into many pieces
in my hand.

Hollie Peploe (9)
Monks Orchard Primary School

Six Ways Of Looking At An Orange

The orange is an orange balloon floating in the air
The orange is a fire flame ready to burst
The orange is a fire flame firing in the air and hitting a window
The orange is an orange football scoring a goal
The orange is a leather circular handbag getting thrown into the air
The orange is a cannonball firing onto a fishing boat.

Alex Clements (8)
Monks Orchard Primary School

Six Ways Of Looking At A Melon

The melon is a giant red and green smily face with bugs on its lips
The melon is a colourful fruit bowl with succulent strawberry juice
The melon is a red sunset reflected by the shiny green sea
                                    with seagulls flying around
The melon is a great tunnel owned by a troll with blood and bones
The melon is a green headband with a red cloak
The melon is a beautiful strange-coloured tiara with bright
                                    onyx twinkles.

Megan Delahunty (9)
Monks Orchard Primary School

Six Ways Of Looking At An Apple

The apple is a big balloon high in the sky
The apple is a beautiful red or green happy face
The apple is a big lovely snack
The apple is as sour as a lemon
The apple is a big red ball getting thrown into the air.

Oliver Bennett (9)
Monks Orchard Primary School

Harvest Festival

The poor people are very happy because we gave them food
                                    and they were very thankful
The leaves are crunching as they are all being swept up
And as they fall from the apple trees standing in the garden
You can touch lots and lots of golden leaves as they crunch
                                    in your soft hands
You should feel relaxed now it's harvest and you see lots of berries
                                    in front of you.

Chloe Upfold (10)
Monks Orchard Primary School

Six Ways Of Looking At A Plum

The plum is a scoop of ice cream freezing in its cone
The plum is like a bowling ball
The plum is like a purple-coloured fish, swimming in the dark blue sea
The plum is a purple bouncy ball
The plum is a red fireball shooting into the sky
The plum is an orange, painted purple.

Harry Riches (8)
Monks Orchard Primary School

Six Ways Of Looking At A Melon

The melon is a ball thrown high in the sky
The melon is as oval-shaped as a baseball
The melon is a green grasshopper jumping
The melon is green as lovely grass
The melon is a pure red inside, really shiny
The melon is a light in the morning.

Okenwa Okonkwo (8)
Monks Orchard Primary School

Five Ways Of Looking At A Lemon

The lemon is a lovely, shiny, smily sun in the sky
The lemon is a yellow ball hanging from the tree
The lemon is a leathery yellow sofa
The lemon is a shape of a rugby ball,
With people playing with it throwing it from side to side
The lemon is a shape of a baby's bottle.

Olwyn O'Gorman (8)
Monks Orchard Primary School

Seven Ways Of Looking At A Carrot

The carrot is a crunchy yummy sweet
The carrot is a massive mountain
The carrot is a pointy sword, singing and glittering
The carrot is a squirt of paint making stains on a chair
The carrot is a piece of grass swaying in the breeze
The carrot is a hockey stick sliding on ice
The carrot is a claw of a tiger slashing people.

Thomas Palmer (8)
Monks Orchard Primary School

Six Ways Of Looking At A Strawberry

The strawberry is a pinky-red rose delicately growing in the garden
The strawberry is a fat sumo wrestler
The strawberry is a bright, shining, red star
The strawberry is as juicy as a gigantic mango
The strawberry is as smelly as perfume
The strawberry is a red, juicy sun smiling in the burning hot weather.

Daniel Bowry (8)
Monks Orchard Primary School

Four Ways Of Looking At A Grape

The grape is a light green stalk growing out of the soft brown soil
The grape is a green stalk, is a pretty rose
The grape is a light green bouncy ball, thrown high into the sweet
blue sky
The grape is a pretty green football that happens to shine lightly.

Shannon Brooker (8)
Monks Orchard Primary School

Three Ways Of Looking At A Kiwi Fruit

The kiwi is a piece of nectar that's lost its petals and will never ever
grow back
The kiwi is a juggling ball as hairy as an old man's chest
The kiwi is a field of grass carved into a ball with some grass trying
to poke out.

Bethany Atkins-Mandell (8)
Monks Orchard Primary School

Four Ways Of Looking At A Melon

A melon is a beam of light that leads to gold and silver
A melon is a ship sailing across the deep blue sea
A melon is a boulder lying on a sandy beach
A melon is a bead lost off a bright yellow necklace.

Elliott Evans (8)
Monks Orchard Primary School

Six Ways Of Looking At A Carrot

The carrot is an orange sausage with spiky hair
The carrot is an orange road with hanging lights
The carrot is a tree with a trunk reflected by the sun
The carrot is a rocket ready for blast-off
The carrot is a fire flame burning pure green grass
The carrot is a long strip of card getting stuck down.

Muhamed Taras (8)
Monks Orchard Primary School

Four Ways Of Looking At A Pineapple

The pineapple is a long prickly hedgehog walking through a dark,
dark cave
The pineapple is a beautiful grain of sand on the lovely beach
The pineapple is a big sun shining in the open sky
The pineapple is a pound of butter melting in a saucepan.

Reshmi Ladwa (8)
Monks Orchard Primary School

Six Ways Of Looking At A Coconut

The coconut is a hairy, dirty, ugly, smelly furball, as hard
as a conker tree
The coconut is an evil pig rolled in black and brown mud
The coconut is a starving hungry bird, eating melted snow inside
The coconut is a land of snowy ice, inside so clear, so cold, so frozen
The coconut is an ice skating ring, famous people ice skating
The coconut is a Horniman museum with hairy, scary, ugly
bugs inside.

Shannon Clarke-Marcelle (8)
Monks Orchard Primary School

Four Ways Of Looking At A Strawberry

The strawberry is as shiny as a red apple
The strawberry is a little love heart flying in the air
The strawberry is a butterfly, the colour is red
The strawberry is an ice cream floating in the sea.

Shannon Elliott (8)
Monks Orchard Primary School

Five Ways Of Looking At A Melon

The melon is a big round ball bounced at playtime
The melon is a big, colourful, juicy, round sphere
The melon is a balloon waiting to be popped and fall down
The melon is a smooth round shell on the beach
The melon is a world with red seas.

Rhiannon Tole (9)
Monks Orchard Primary School

Evacuation

My mum was crying wishes to me
The whistle blew
I got on the train, I wondered how long I would be there
My heart was pounding
I was thinking, *will he have a vicious dog?*
Would it be someone who molests people?
I was standing in a line
Waiting for a tag with my name on to put on my braces
Finally the lady came by
I had a lump in my throat
It was very hard to swallow
I went to sit down
I was wondering what he would be like
I jumped up as the whistle blew
The billet officer said,
'We're here.' Everyone was getting off the train
My friends were looking at the green grass and the river
I could feel a cold breeze
I could see the church
The officer took me to my destination.

Alexander Stewart (10)
Monks Orchard Primary School

Evacuation

Priest praying quietly to a small crowd
Devastation looks on pale faces
Children consume food as if it's their last supper
Sneezing infants that are suffering from dust
Children screaming because they don't want to be evacuated
as if they are dying
I stand on the platform, as still as can be, like I'm a statue
I see crying children
I wonder as if I've never wondered before
Staring into the foggy sky, thinking, *will they harm me?*
Do they have kids?
The obese billeting officer gives everyone name tags
As if they are parcels and packages
Gradually I step onto the train
I sit down on contaminated seats
I stuff myself in the seat
Petrified I look around
I hold in my breath, pinch my nose
A fat chubby boy is eating lots of food
Vomits everywhere, it's *noxious!*
Let out a deep breath, let go of my nose
I start wheezing, I can feel pain and sorrow in my heart
My heart is pounding like charging elephants
My face is frozen, I shiver in shock
My face breaks into rolling drops of tears
I want to cry, I just can't
The annoying whistle goes
On this occasion, it's because the train's slowing down
Arriving safely in the warmth of the countryside.

Roshan Roberts (10)
Monks Orchard Primary School

The Blitz

I awoke from my midnight dream
To hear the sound of sirens echoing through my head
I heard the heavy thud of bombs crashing onto the ground
I was so scared - I thought I was going to die
I felt so nervous and cold my heart was beating heavily like a stone
I rushed outside to hear the explosions
But it emerged there were none to be heard
I ventured a bit further to see if my house was still standing
But when I looked I didn't see anything
All I saw was a pile of bricks.

Joshua Lartey (11)
Monks Orchard Primary School

The Blitz

Hearing the sirens again and again
I sprinted outside in the pouring rain
In the shelter it's cold and damp
I wanted to escape
But it wouldn't be safe
We're all like animals stuck in an enclosure
But suddenly, I heard an explosion
We waited fearfully
Then went out
The area was still
Until a baby broke the silence
I stare in horror
I see my old house burning
I burst into tears
Cuddle my mum
Feeling anxious and upset
I can't stop thinking about the bombs
I want to be evacuated
But I know it's too late
I'm lonely and afraid
Helpless.

Laura McCarthy (10)
Monks Orchard Primary School

The Blitz

Sleeping in my bed I heard an ear-crackling sound
I knew something was wrong, I didn't know what it was
We raced to the bottom of the garden and went into a metal shed
Mum said, 'Let's play a game,'
I didn't know what was going to happen to my surroundings
Then it started to get worse, I heard crashing and vibrations under
my feet
My sister was crying, she was scared of the bangs
I finally got to sleep again
I woke up and the devastation had finished
We went outside to see the devastation
Beyond us people were screaming and shouting
And my house was a wreck.

Daniel Harris (11)
Monks Orchard Primary School

The Blitz

I woke up from a midnight dream
To hear the sounds of sirens
I looked out of my window
To see shocked faces
As London died in ruins
All my family ran to the air raid shelter
To make sure we were all safe
Anger, devastation, all different emotions
Hit me
How long could we be in here?
A week or maybe forever
I wish this could end.

Thomas Kallas (10)
Monks Orchard Primary School

Evacuation

As I stomp on the train
I want to cry
There's a lump in my throat
Like a pill that won't move
As the whistle blows
Off we go.

As I enter the countryside
I see green grass and flowers
As the train comes to a stop
I feel even more uptight
What will my billet be like?
Will I get the belt?

We are picked up from the town hall
I am fifth to go
My billet is pleasing
And her name is Miss Foe.

My room is dusty
And it's very small
It is very cosy
And not very tall.

I hope I'm going home soon
I really miss my mum
As a tear trickles down my face
I go into a fluster.

Lauren Trout (11)
Monks Orchard Primary School

Evacuation

It was time to go
Now the sirens had blown
Will never stop until the end.

I was all alone
I was scared of fear
No one will even come near.

I got off the train
And tried not to fall down the gap
But for some reason, I could hear a tap.

Then I saw the billeting officer
She was so obese
She almost fell at my feet.

I followed her with the others
We were scared of where we were going to go
We went one by one.

I was the last one to be dropped off
But I didn't care
When I got there he started to ruin my hair.

A few days later I threatened his dog
I was so happy, I didn't get a smack
But I could still hear that tap.

It was time to go, it was a dream come true
But when I got on the train I felt the winter blues
The train stopped, I got off to see my mum
She slapped me and called me a fool!

I went home with depression, I felt upset
Then she sent me to my bed, now I wish I was dead!

Jobi Freeman-Lampard (10)
Monks Orchard Primary School

Evacuation

I'm so nervous
I'm not sure
Where I'm going
Why I'm going?

I'm missing my family already
I've got a pain in my tummy
I'm worried too
I don't know what to do.

Mums and dads
Surrounding me
My mum's at home
Not with me.

I hear a train
Come to a halt
I need to hurry
I have to climb on.

Everyone scrambles on
Except me
I see a girl
She glances at me.

The first thing I notice is
The choking smoke
I can't bear it
I start to splutter.

The next thing I know
I hear a loud mutter
We are finally here
We are so nervous
I just can't bear it.

Danielle Addison (11)
Monks Orchard Primary School

Evacuation!

All alone, off we go to the countryside
No brothers, no sisters to help me through the night
I am as scared as a fish is of a shark
No one to get me through the dark.

All aboard, off we go
To a place I never want to go
Some people say, 'No good.'
Some people say, 'I want no food.'

Around comes the lady with the tray
Knowing no one will buy today
Wasting her breath on the kids
Until someone finally slid
Into the back of her and the tray
Only to cry and pray and pray.

Off we come
Looking for someone
Finally find the billeting officer
Now we're going to our billet
Then the kind man gives me some fish fillet.

The bed is wet
And his silly pet
Is scratching my leg
Making me beg and beg.

Now I'm enjoying it
Hoping and waiting to stay a bit.

Anthony Young (10)
Monks Orchard Primary School

Evacuation

Clambering onto the train a lump appears in my throat
Like a pill that won't budge
The whistle of the train burns through me
Like a hole in the head
The steam chokes me as the train pulls away
Out of sight I go
The chug of the train burns through my body
Until I feel sick.

I arrive at the station
All alone, but not safe
Strangers everywhere
What do I do?
'Stay away,' I shout
And I run to the billeting officer.

Atlanta Gunstone (10)
Monks Orchard Primary School

Evacuation

Everyone says goodbye to their mum or dad
But now I have to go
The train leaves the station,
A tear rolls down my cheek
Mum and Dad . . . I miss you already
I'm feeling ill, I vomit
My brother reassures me
'It's just for a week and two days.'

Taylor May (10)
Monks Orchard Primary School

Zebras

A zebra has stripes,
The white is for day
And black is for night
And they don't bite
It would see you but, try to hide
Zebras are scared of lions
And they would run for their lives.

Namirah Anderson (7)
Monks Orchard Primary School

Apple

An apple is red and green
Peel it and eat it
Picked from a tree
Like football players
You will become healthy
Eat an apple every day.

Michael Greaves (7)
Monks Orchard Primary School

The Banana

The banana is as yellow as a daffodil
The banana is as silky as a statue
The banana is as soft as a teddy bear
The banana is from Africa
The banana is as silky as a box
The banana is as squashy as a pillow.

Chloe Scott (8)
Monks Orchard Primary School

Pets

I really have three pets,
I don't even know what to call them.

I have a monkey, a pig and a chinchilla,
It is quite embarrassing I have hairs all over
One of the worst times of the day
Is what my Mum calls walkie time,
Everybody in the street looks at me with weird eyes.

The thing I hate most is bath night for all three of my pets
It's like running the marathon, backwards, forwards I go
Getting towels, shampoo and combs
But there is a thing to look forward to
In the day it is bedtime: calm, relaxing and without my *pets!*

Then guess what happens in the middle
At the stroke of midnight?
My chinchilla comes running for a . . . bed for the night!

Ellen Dickinson (9)
St Catherine's Prep School, Guildford

Old And New

There was a little girl that said,
'I hate pollution, I wish I could go back in time
I hate factories, they make pollution, cars do too, even mine!
That's what makes global warming
And now all the ice is melting at the North and South poles
It's a warning.'
So she walked and she walked to the witch's house
The witch said,
'What do you want, oh what do you want, oh what do you want?'
'I want to go back in time, not to the Stone Age though.'
The witch said, 'I'll give it a go.'
So the little girl went back in time
And taught the children in stories and mime
That pollution was bad, it would melt all the ice
And, 'I can tell you, pollution's not nice!'

Gabrielle Puleston-Vaudrey (7)
Seaton House School

How I Wanted It So Much

Dad said I couldn't keep a tortoise
He said I couldn't keep a hare
I couldn't even keep a big, fat, grizzly bear.

How I wanted it so much.

Dad said I couldn't keep a rabbit
He said I couldn't keep a bat
I couldn't even keep a small, nice, cuddly cat.

How I wanted it so much.

Dad said I couldn't keep a fox
He said I couldn't keep a hedgehog
I couldn't even keep a big, fat, croaky frog.

How I wanted it so much
Hey look, a small cuddly mouse
I had something all along
Snap!
There goes the mousetrap.

Onyeka Ambrose (9)
Seaton House School

The Circus

Lights turn on,
Crowds cheer
Suddenly circus stars appear

First the clowns
With funny hair
Cycling, juggling everywhere

Acrobats jumping high
Monkeys on the beam
It's time for some ice cream.

Olivia Keen (8)
Seaton House School

Horses Everywhere

H orses are lively animals
O n the hills horses play
R oan, black and chestnut colour
S ee them galloping, neighing with delight
E ach horse a different shape and size
S ome horses stay all night

E arly to rise in their stables
V ery small horses try to reach up to the gate
E ager horses put their heads out for sugar lumps
R eins and saddles hanging up
Y ou can see horses showjumping
W ild horses run in the west of America
H ere they eat on the plains
E verywhere people like horses
R iding round the circus ring
E verywhere horses are seen.

Felicity Goldsack (9)
Seaton House School

Sunday

Sunday mornings are such fun
Staying in bed till half past one
Under the duvet
What will I do today?
I'll play with my hamster
Play with my cat
Play with my friend
I hope the day will never end
But very soon it's time for bed
And I must be ready for the week ahead
I'll work hard every day
I just can't wait for . . . *Sunday!*

Emily Gibson (9)
Seaton House School

Seasons

Spring can be hot,
It can also be cold,
All the animals are born
And the flowers unfold
Beautiful, beautiful, beautiful.

Summer is hot,
No wind in the air
You can go in the pool
Or sit in your deckchair
Sun, sun, sun.

Autumn is when
The red leaves fall
The brightness is fading
And the weather is cool
Leaves, leaves, leaves.

Winter is cold
All the colours have gone
It is so much fun in the snow
It's the last season
Cold, cold, cold.

All the seasons are great
They are all different
I always enjoy
Thinking of the best moment
Seasons, seasons, seasons.

Laura Hutchins (10)
Seaton House School

At The Beach

At the beach it is so much fun,
Playing in the sand so soft and golden.
Building sandcastles,
Finding shells and digging deep holes.

Playing in the sea can be cold,
But there are so many things to do
Swimming, floating on lilos, water skiing
But the best part is jumping through the waves!

The sea is deep and is a turquoise colour,
The waves roll and crash against the rocks and shore,
Bringing with it slimy green seaweed,
Which tangles around your feet.

There are so many different types of fish in the sea,
Angelfish, catfish, sharks and whales
The dolphin is the most spectacular
Jumping through the waves.

There are big boats, little boats,
People going on cruise ships on holiday,
Fishermen casting their nets from little fishing boats
Then they take their fish home for their tea.

Lucy Tarran (10)
Seaton House School

Dogs

Dogs, dogs all over the place
Some like to pout and some like to race
You've got a Labrador, an Airedale too
Somehow a lot like you.

Dogs, dogs all over the place
Some evil people put them in a case
Luckily we've got the RSPCA
They've rescued so many dogs in one day.

Little puppies are so cute
They bark like little flutes
Running, jumping, having fun
Little puppies love to run
All this laughter, happiness and play
Is just one small doggy day.

Dogs are cute, dogs are fun
Yorkshire Terriers are number one.

King Charles spaniels
Are so small
But can I tell you, the best of all
The best of all who wins all over the rest
Means Airedale terriers are the best.

Dogs are cute, who is fun
Labradors, hey I want one.

Michelle Thompson (10)
Seaton House School

The Circus

There were clowns, jugglers and tightrope walkers too
And with them they brought monkeys, apes and baboons.

They put up the tent and opened the door,
We sat down to watch as they marched across the floor.

The jugglers started juggling, the clowns started their act,
The tightrope walkers balanced, sure-footed as a cat.

Then a monkey stole a juggling ball and then the clown's flower
And took a run up, leapt into the air and landed on the ape tower.

The ape tower trembled and collapsed onto the floor,
All of the audience walked out of the door.

The circus packed up and said their goodbyes,
Then left the tent with gloomy faces and sighs.

Goodbye jugglers, clowns and tightrope walkers too
And monkeys and apes, don't forget the baboons.

Gemma Hutton (10)
Seaton House School

Associations

Character, book, police, jail,
Bar, chocolate, money, sale,
Bargain, haggle, argue, cross,
Nought, number, minus, loss.
Win, match, pair, shoes,
Walk, travel, sail, cruise,
Deck, captain, sailor, male,
Character, book, police, jail.

Felicity O'Toole (10)
Seaton House School

Associations

Lucky, clover, butter, cake,
Ice, cold, winter, snowflake,
Unique, person, kid, goat,
Cheese, dairy, milk, float,
Parade, costume, play, fun,
Happy, smile, mouth, bun,
Hair, head, brain, smart,
Suit, tie, ribbon, art,
Sew, needle, prick, thorn,
Rose, flower, pick, corn,
Crop, farmer, grow, take,
Lucky, clover, butter, cake.

Annabelle Anyi Wang (10)
Seaton House School

Cup Cakes

Cup cakes, cup cakes
Ever so scrummy
I believe they should live
In my tum, tum, tummy.

Cup cakes, cup cakes
I need some more
Maybe they're hidden
In my bottom drawer.

I look in the drawer,
But hey, there are no more
Cup cakes, cup cakes
Ever so sad
Now all I am is very, very mad!

Georgina Howard (10)
Thames Ditton Junior School

Be Happy

Always remember be happy not sad,
Because you will spoil the fun,
Other things will hurt you more,
Like staying too long in the sun.

They say it was so hard to smile,
They say it doesn't matter,
But let's ignore their silly chatter,
And always try to flatter.

If you had a great achievement,
You'd have the mood to be happy,
But if you were feeling snappy,
Everyone around is flappy!

If you've won a competition,
You'd be over the moon,
But if it happens too soon,
Go and buy a silver spoon.

If something you see is funny,
You can have a little laugh,
But all I ask of you is this,
Please do not be daft.

Happy, happy, happy,
What a snappy rhyme,
It's easy to be happy,
But not all the time.

Elizabeth Monaghan (8)
Thames Ditton Junior School

Eternity

Why does life have to be eternal?
Why can't it be just a short while?
Maybe it's just the ways of time,
But in this time, existed crime.

Why oh why is the world full of evil?
I wish all villains would just stand still
But these are my thoughts, why should you care?
You just sit there, without a care.

And now I come to the end of this chat,
But please don't fret,
I'll be back,
But not yet.

Giovanni Cornell-Lombardo (11)
Thames Ditton Junior School

My Teddy Bear

I have a teddy bear and it has a ribbon in its hair
I give it food and give it lots of care
It has a pink nose and it likes to have a doze
I even go out and give it lots of clothes
I like to go to the park with it
And she likes to sit on my lap while I knit
I was watching TV with her and suddenly I heard a purr
I looked under my feet and who did I meet?
A cat - I was very annoyed with it
It was chewing my hat.

Alice Ridsdale (8)
Thames Ditton Junior School

My Moon Poem

Moon, the wonderful moon, how brightly you shine
I love you so and I am glad you are mine
I love to see you change your shape, from half to full
When I go outside I see your reflection in the pool
I wish I could go and see you more closely
Because you are the one I know about mostly.

Erin Cummins (7)
Thames Ditton Junior School

Love Is . . .

Love is bright, love is dark
Maybe sometimes they give you a mark
Love is nice, love is bad
But whatever happens, don't be mad
Love is cute, love is ugly
But together your lovely love
Brings the world together.

David Cornell-Lombardo (9)
Thames Ditton Junior School

Floss

My guinea pig's called Floss
She is big and ginger
She thinks that she is the boss
Sometimes she bites my finger.

Georgia Imrie (10)
Thames Ditton Junior School

Birthdays

Birthdays, birthdays,
All around,
Laughing, giggling
It's the only sound.

Parties everywhere
On the land
And on the beaches
In the sand.

Seeing children
Scream and shout
Lots of groups
All about.

We all love
To celebrate
Especially when
We're turning eight.

Georgina Pearson (7)
Thames Ditton Junior School

Lunchtime

Lunchtime, lunchtime
I'm feeling so hungry
I could eat a cheeky monkey.

Hannah Phelps (8)
Thames Ditton Junior School

Flowers

Flowers are pretty just for you,
Flowers can be pink, red, violet or blue,
Flowers have pollen that can make you sneeze,
Flowers are pollinated by insects like wasps and bees.

Some seeds grow into flowers and that is true,
Flowers are especially pretty, when they are new
Flowers are great!

Kerry Alderson (10)
Thames Ditton Junior School

Mum And Me

Mum says, 'I'm naughty,'
And I am!
Mum says, 'I'm cheeky,'
And I am!
Mum says, 'I'm silly.'
And I am!
Mum says, 'She loves me.'
And I love her too!

Heather Alderson (7)
Thames Ditton Junior School

My Cats

Cats can . . .
Curl and leap
They can spring and run
They can lick and twirl and twirl
They can miaow and purr
What do you think of cats?

Catherine Coxeter-Smith (7)
Thames Ditton Junior School

Thames Ditton Junior School

At Thames Ditton Junior School we read and write
Until it's late at night
Then morning comes when we feel bright
I hope the teacher won't take fright
At school we tuck our shirts in to look smart
But most of all I like art.
Our faces fall when the teacher says, 'It's test time, hurry up.'
I have to go and feed my pup
After school we go to dance club
We spring and sway until we touch the ground
When I get home I am tired and sleepy
So I take a little nap.

Sarah Macmillan (8)
Thames Ditton Junior School

My Whale Poem

The blue whale swam slowly in the shiny water
The smooth whale jumped quickly over the wavy water
The big shiny whale swam for miles in the deep blue sea
The big blue whale.

The bumpy whale spurted water out of his blowhole
The plankton disappears into the whale's huge, dark, slimy mouth
The big blue whale.

Amy Horner (8)
Thames Ditton Junior School

If I Just Knew . . .

If I just knew how to save the mountains
If I just knew how to save the trees
If I just knew how to save the animals
Oh, that would make me so happy.

Alice Harmer (7)
Thames Ditton Junior School

Secret Snihplod

Shh, it's a secret!
Shh, it's a secret!
Can you keep a secret?
It's a good one!
I will tell you
I'll describe it - shall I?

An animal, an animal and an animal it is
Different colours they can be
Spotty, sparkly, freckly
Lives in water, warm and cold
Warm-blooded animal.

Wriggles, wiggles, wallows
Like a slimy snake, slithering through the undergrowth
My beautiful creature, seems so grand with its streamline shape
A beaked snout, like an arching bow.

Its eyes are coal-coloured, pebble-like look
Sleek, thin, fan-like blue fins
Blue and grey as the sky
Have you guessed the secret?
A dolphin!

Morgan Burne (8)
Thames Ditton Junior School

Me And The BFG

I looked out the window and what did I see
I saw a big giant called BFG
He looked at me strangely and I thought he was dainty
He had a golden trumpet
And had a scratch where he bumped it
I said, 'Bye-bye,' he started to cry
'I am going to miss you,' he said,
'When you go back to bed.'

Hannah Ridsdale (8)
Thames Ditton Junior School

The Stars

Twinkling above us,
Elamin and her friends
Light up the world at night
Like a dance that never ends.

Shooting star, make a wish
And it will come true
Like if you want your day of school to end
Or if you want to cheer up your friend who is blue.

Zoë Barr (9)
Thames Ditton Junior School

Big Dogs

Big dogs
Little dogs
Clever dogs
Stupid dogs

Fast dogs
Slow dogs
Thin dogs
Fat dogs

Cute dogs
Scary dogs
Hairy dogs
Lairy dogs

Stripy dogs
Fluffy dogs
Golden dogs
Spotty dogs

All dogs
Every dog
Man's best friend.

Natasha Thomas (8)
Thames Ditton Junior School

The Sound Of Animals

The sound of horses' hooves
The scratch from a tabby cat
The noise of a woodpecker going *tap, tap, tap.*

The whine of a very cute puppy
The buzzing of a bumblebee
The pitter-patter of feet as the squirrel climbs the tree.

The hissing of the snake
The cry of a fox
The chirping of a robin in its bird box.

The rustling of a badger
The squeak from a mouse
The screech of an owl flying over a house.

Emily Godwin (10)
The Raleigh School

Blackberries

Black and bulgy, round and sweet
Juicy and yummy, oh the things I like to eat

In my mind I munch and chew
I really cannot wait
Juice oozing from my mouth
These berries tastes so great!

Glossy fat blackberries
Ripening in the sun
Going to eat them all today
Every single one.

Too many blackberries
My tummy's very sore
But I am sure when tomorrow comes
I will eat some more!

Imogen Heenan (10)
The Raleigh School

My Best Friend

My best friend is the bestest friend anyone could have
She is funny, kind, sweet and cute
Well my best friend is the funniest of all and better than yours
Actually my best friend is the greatest, she's rich and most of all cool
If you think yours is so great wait until I tell you about mine . . .
This goes on every playtime I just stand there and watch at the back
But I actually know who's best friend is the greatest
And at all of those things . . . mine!

Ellie Byrne (10)
The Raleigh School

My Cat

She pounces as she takes down her prey
She wakes me up in the morning, by the lick of her tongue
She's adorable in every single way
I love her and she loves me
She sleeps by my feet in bed
I am the luckiest person in the world
And I love her to bits
That's my cat!

Eleanor Wood (10)
The Raleigh School

Escape

Sometimes I need to escape,
So I wrap myself in a cape.
All I can see is darkness,
Which is less and less.
But most of all I like the quiet,
So I can't hear the riot,
That is going on!

Laura Douet (10)
The Raleigh School

I'm Bored

'Mum, what can I do?'
'Well, why don't you play with your train set?'
'Already played with that.'
'OK, why don't you play with Dodger the dog?'
'Already played with him.'
'What haven't you played with in your room?'
'Dunno, I'm just bored!'
'Why don't you play with your fish?'
'Don't want to.'
'Find a way to amuse yourself but don't ask me.'

Nicholas Allen (10)
The Raleigh School

I Had A Little Brother

I had a little brother
He's as annoying as can be

I had a little brother
He messes up my room

I had a little brother
Who makes a lot of noise

I had a little brother
Who says he's a winner

I had a little brother
Who is actually very nice.

Jemma Daniel (7)
The Raleigh School

Autumn

At the crack of dawn you get up
The window is misted with morning dew
You get out of bed and thrust on your clothes and warm cosy jacket
And rush outside to see the green spiky conker shells fall with a plop.

They lie waiting, the smoothest, shiniest conkers you have ever seen
The orange, golden leaves
Fall and twirl to the ground
Making a carpet of leaves under the trees.

Darkness creeps in as you crawl up to bed
You are extremely tired from the day that just passed
I love autumn.

Katy Nicholls (10)
The Raleigh School

Friends

Friends are special
Sometimes made of metal
This may sound weird.

But it is very true
If some person is rude to you
Your friend is always there.

So friends are the best
And together you can rest
And be friends forever and ever.

Eve Hurcombe (10)
The Raleigh School

Changing Seasons

Autumn leaves shaded gold or brown
Can make a smile out of a frown
Bright colours are gone in a dash
While the rays of the sun disappear in a flash.

A winter's moon like frosted rings
Still there when you listen to what the milkman sings
Droplets stained on the web of a spider
That makes the winter tough, with cold droplets beside her.

Spring type blossom upon the trees
Always seems to attract the bees
Small birds sweetly singing
While you faintly hear the church bells ringing.

The summer scent is in the air
There's now no more cold weather to bear
Then the sun sets below the water's surprises
And tomorrow above the cliffs it rises.

So many things happen during our seasons
And those things happen for many good reasons.

Megan Keepence (10)
The Raleigh School

Smiley Faces

Smiley faces may look sad
When you hurt them pretty bad
Smiley faces may look happy
When you see a baby's nappy.

Connor Paton (10)
The Raleigh School

Animal Park

Silent snakes slowly
Slithering through leaf litter
Lively lions lying on the floor
Fruit bats bursting, different fruits.

Wild warthogs running for prey
Whilst kung-fu cats chase the prey away
Stalking Siberian tigers sleeping
Snoozing for the day.

Slippery snails sliming the way
Creepy spiders making their web
Whilst swinging monkeys swing away
The limas leave for the day.

Tall giraffes, tall and proud
Tiny ants, small and sad
Elephants walking and being loud
Laughing hyenas going mad.

Slow slugs, slow as can be
As bumblebees bursting pollen, sucking it up
Howler monkeys happily howling
Black, orange tigers bite like the people say.

Will Mead (9)
The Raleigh School

The Big Bad Teacher

There once was a big bad teacher
She was very strict
She went to my school
And said, 'Have a picnic.'
At first I thought she was nice
But then she picked up a chair
And you will not believe it
She did it to my class again.

Freya Casserly (8)
The Raleigh School

Nature

The olive-coloured vines wrapping around big trees
Chestnut branches breaking in the very strong breeze
Trees growing quickly to reach the bright sky
Brown leaves being blown away so very high
Different coloured leaves lying on the grassy floor
A few drops of rain turning to a downpour.

Murray Hampshire (9)
The Raleigh School

Life At The Park

Flowers smell sweet, pink, purple, blue,
Stream has gunk looks like goo
Sweet smell of ending summer
Bamboo leaves with no lovely colour
A sea of trees elevated so high
Birds are flying high in the sky
Crunching leaves under your feet
Might not be much heat
Don't panic animals still eat
That's one day at the park
A cold day at the park
A cold day at the park
That's one day at the park.

Running about comes a boy scout
Trampling over the plants
Here comes a rat, all sleek and fat
Nibbling at the plants
Up a tree goes a bee
To get to a tasty treat
In the summer there's a surprise round every corner
That's one day at the park
A hot day at the park
A hot day at the park
That's one day at the park.

Bradley Conisbee (9)
The Raleigh School

The Amazing Rainforest

Monkeys swing from tree to tree
Cheetahs running with so much glee
Birds soaring in the night sky
Tigers on the hunt with a glint in their eye

As hot as a greenhouse on a summer's day
Rain in the air like a misty spray
Trees all around as tall as towers
Decorated with lots of flowers

This is a place of magic and wisdom
God's creatures in their kingdom
Gorillas run free and wild
What an amazing place for a child.

Scott Spencer (9)
The Raleigh School

Tour Of The Desert

In the desert there is . . .
A cactus boiling in the sun
Spikes dry, prickling anyone
Snakes shining, flying around
Spiders nasty on the ground.

Bugs small, scuttling by
Ants collecting leaves, dry
Look, an oasis over there
And dunes scattered everywhere.

An occasional camel plodding along
Maroon canyons echoing a gong
And some dangerous sandstorms raging around
Oh look, a lizard on the ground.

And that shows the desert's ups and downs.

Alexander Worsfold (9)
The Raleigh School

Below The Canopy

Monkeys brown, swing from tree to tree
Whilst birds are flying high
Making nests on branches
Which reach up in the sky.
Leaves green, dripping with rain
Flowing into a stream
Silvery, so silvery, shining with gleam.
Parrots, colourful in the sky
Swooping and squawking
Perched in the tree up high.
Gorillas, brown and hairy
Swing through the hot and humid air
Over palm trees and banana trees
Back to their leafy lair.
Frogs, smooth as well as shiny
Jumping around the stream,
Up and down on the leaves
Like little bouncing beads.

Rachel Butcher (9)
The Raleigh School

Animals

Some big, some small
Some fat, some tall
Every size, every kind
I like them all, I don't mind.
I like the cat, I like the dog
I even like the little green frog
Horses, rabbits, little field mice
I like all animals, they are all nice.

Phoebe Davies (10)
The Raleigh School

My Magic Box

(Based on 'Magic Box' by Kit Wright)

I will put in the box . . .
The two spirits of my cats that died
The love of my great, great grandma
The taste of melting chocolate.

I will put in the box . . .
The feel of Sophie's long hair
The smell of petrol
The love of my aunt and uncle.

I will put in my box . . .
The taste of sugary sweets
The great coral reef
Lots of glimmering pearls.

My box is to be made of shiny gold
With shiny blue dolphins.

Gina Dyce (7)
The Raleigh School

Garden In Spring

Vast green lawns lined
With neat rustling hedgerows
Or flower beds bobbing with blooming flowers
Blossoming trees waving fruit-covered boughs
At a beautiful clear blue sky
A shimmering pond with multi-sized pond-skaters
Skimming across the water
Golden carp gobbling at the surface
A vegetable patch with vegetables full
From pointy carrots to runner beans
And to finish you off, here's a tip:
Don't let pollen get on your lip.

Robert Peel (9)
The Raleigh School

Animals In The Rainforest

I see the orange and black-striped tiger prowling round the rainforest
I see scarlet frogs jumping across the water
I see slithering snakes smelling the olive leaves
I see loud brown monkeys jumping from tree to tree
I see harmless snails sliding, slowly across the forest floor
All this I see in my dream.

Dominic Brown (9)
The Raleigh School

On The Rainforest Floor

A shining black python slithering
In the moonlight a silver parrot flying
The spout of a trunk reaching for sunlight
Brown leaves composting
Beautiful tree frogs jumping wild
Scarlet fruit falling to the ground
Yellow tigers stalking for prey
The aqua water dripping softly
Tasty fungi burrowing their roots
The wonderful rainforest is at its best
Improving, dying and growing.

Emily Broome (9)
The Raleigh School

In The Garden

Diamond-coloured water dripping off leaves
Flowers, maroon, still as could ever be
Fish, colourful, splashing in the cold water
All types of things I like to see

Bees bright, buzzing everywhere
Green grass whooshing in the air
Brown mud squelching under wellies
This is what I like to hear.

Ellie Punshon (9)
The Raleigh School

Labrador Rap

I wanna tell you about a dog called Jessie
Unlike other dogs she ain't that messy
When I take her on walks she goes a bit wild
Fetching sticks, playful as a child
She loves to chase a rabbit or startle a pheasant
But if she caught one it wouldn't be pleasant
Back at base, she's full of playful growling
And we're all thankful that she don't do howling
When the family hugs, she wants to join in
Whining like a baby till we have to give in
She'll climb on the sofa and chew our socks
I suppose it's bad, but I think she rocks
She's black, she's soft, she's one of a kind
She's simply the best dog you'll ever find.

Clemmy Hill (10)
The Raleigh School

The Rainforest

Squawking, howling, rustling and croaking
These are the sounds of the rainforest.
Frogs, birds, monkeys and lizards
These are the animals of the rainforest.
Nuts, fruits, oils and spices
These are the foods from the rainforest.
Red, green, yellow and blue
These are the colours of the rainforest.
Tall, small, wide and thin
These are the trees of the rainforest.
Fresh air, medicine, food and more
These are what we need the rainforest for.
Roads, diggers, axes and saws,
These are destroying the rainforest
Stop the destruction!

Daniel Steeden (10)
The Raleigh School

Jack, Sam And Lily!

Jack, Sam and Lily
They are cute and cuddly
And full of spots

Whenever they're with me
They make me smile
They're full of fun and full of glee
My mum says that one of them
Is just like me
Cheeky little characters
Always fun and free.

Chloe Holland (10)
The Raleigh School

Joys In Life

Summer's touch
Winter's bite
The light of day
The dead of night.

The green of grass
The white of snow
Mother Earth
I love you so.

Friends, family, pets and all
Come around, we'll have a ball
Bring the goods of life along
We'll celebrate in joyful song.

Niall O'Hara (11)
The Raleigh School

The Funniest Thing I Ever Saw Was . . .

The funniest thing I ever saw was . . .
An elephant getting up from the floor.

The funniest thing I ever saw was . . .
Daddy banging his head on the door.

The funniest thing I ever saw was . . .
A lion doing a funky dance.

The funniest thing I ever saw was . . .
A pencil doing press-ups on the floor.

The funniest thing I ever saw was . . .
A hippo having a manicure.

The funniest thing I ever saw was . . .
A puppy dog waving its paw.

Ellie Bonwick (7)
The Raleigh School

My Best Friend

She is sweet, she is kind
But watch out, what you say to her
She tends to speak her mind.

Sometimes she is bossy
But not in a nasty way
But hey, she's still the greatest friend.

She is lovely and she's gorgeous
She's mad and oh so funny
Always glad, she's never sad
That's why she's my best *buddy!*

April Saunders (10)
The Raleigh School

Fish Fun

Goldfish glisten
Zooming in the tank
Dolphins sparkle
Skimming across the ocean
Jellyfish glow
Pumping forwards in darkness
Sharks terrify
Racing across the sea
Pufferfish expand
Trundling in the water
Sea horses shine
Fluttering their fins across the ocean's floor.

Aaron Henderson (10)
The Raleigh School

My Pets!

My pets are cute and cuddly
My pets are sweet and fluffy
I love them lots and lots.

My pets are at the top
So give me a . . .
P
Give me an . . .
E
Give me a . . .
TS
Pets!

Emily Clifford (10)
The Raleigh School

Things To Remember For Christmas

There's cold in the air and Christmas is in December
And here's some things that you should remember

If you have a sister, make sure you don't sit on her
If you have some brothers, don't fight with them others

If aunts and uncles come to your door
Don't shout out that they are a bore
And if your grandparents you visit
Sit still and don't fidget

Cos there's frost in the air and Christmas is in December
And here's more things for you to remember

When you go to school, don't act like a fool
And if to church you go, don't trudge along real slow

If your friend brings a card, don't hit him real hard
And if you see Santa, don't annoy him with banter

Cos there's snow in the air and Christmas is in December
And here's one final thing for you to remember

Your parents will love you forever, so don't say to them, 'Whatever.'
They don't like it when you're bad, cos it makes them really sad.

So, a good kid you should be and lots of presents you'll see
When you wake up and you're yawning on a beautiful
                              Christmas morning

Cos there's smiles everywhere and maybe snow on the ground
And wherever you look, there's happiness all around.

Mitchell Robinson (9)
The Raleigh School

My Perfect Day!

My perfect day would start with breakfast in bed - bacon, egg and toast
Shopping next with all my friends to see who can spend the most
Afterwards we'd go to the amusement arcade, to spend
                                    some more money
Then swimming with the pool to ourselves, that would be really funny
I would end my day going bowling with my family and I'd get
                                    the highest score
And finish off with a giant pizza and eat till we couldn't eat anymore.

Rebecca Witherspoon (10)
The Raleigh School

England Versus Croatia

It was England vs Croatia
Upon that foreign turf
All down to eleven men
To show what they were worth.

But, England, England, England
What a dreadful team
Quite the worst performance
We have ever seen.

It was poor concentration by Robinson
That started the downhill trend
He let in two careless goals
His career should surely end.

England, England, England
What an unpleasant sight
Heads were lower than the grass
Robinson's face was white.

England, England, England
Croatia seemed to wreck 'em
Things will soon get better
If we send for Beckham!

Matthew Mole (9)
The Raleigh School

My Relative

I need to tell you about my relative,
My relative is rather strange.
You see he likes to live in trees,
And he . . . he is sometimes deranged.
He can't do the subjects we learn about,
But intelligent he is.
He likes to leap and bound,
He is not like my cousin Liz.
He is not a little cousin,
Or an uncle who is funky.
No he is not a very active grandpa,
He is our relative, the *monkey!*

Dillon Millington (9)
The Raleigh School

My Nanny

In the summer holidays
It was fantastic fun
We went to my nan's house
And played giant games in the sun.
My nan is really helpful
She really likes to make
Lots of lovely dresses
She's fab for goodness sake.
My nan has got small cell cancer
She is suffering from it
We will be there for her
For every single bit.
I really love my nanny
She is really kind
Please come on and meet her
She has a lovely mind.

Emily Merry (9)
The Raleigh School

The Girl Who Sat On The Stair

There was a girl who sat on a stair
Dreaming about fantasy things
Like beautiful dresses and lovely princesses
Who wore diamond beads and rings.

There was a girl who sat on a stair
Dreaming about fantasy things
Like daring knights who won battles and fights
Also proud, magnificent kings.

One day the girl from the stair
Became a poet who wrote about things
Like beautiful dresses and lovely princesses
who wore diamond beads and rings
Like daring knights who won battles and fights
Also proud, magnificent kings.

Monika Smith (9)
The Raleigh School

When The Builders Came

When the builders came they made loads of noise
They brought machinery that they used like toys.

They took out the walls and jack-hammered the floor
Knocked through the ceilings and dismantled the doors.

The house has been taken away in large skips
There is not much left, just some small concrete bits.

I'm hoping one day that our house will return
For this loss of a home is quite a concern.

William Schaale (9)
The Raleigh School

Famous People

Famous people have lots of money
And full of lots of passion
Most of them are as sweet as honey
But all are full of fashion
Some of them like to sing
And some do not
All the boys like to wear bling
And all of the girls are hot
Most of them have lots of talent
Some of them I see every day
I think all the dancers have lots of balance
Along with all their pay
I like pets and they do too
Cats and dogs and many more
So many pets it looks like a zoo
And on television lots I saw
So that is all I know.

Ellen Phillpot (9)
The Raleigh School

Football Goal

I duck
I pass the ball
He shoots
And it is a throw-in
I get it
I dodge
I sprint
I shoot
It is a goal
I cheer.

Jonathan Finch (9)
The Raleigh School

Fame

The catwalk is waiting, the people are here
The clock is ticking, the time is near
Just walk out, strut your stuff
Then do a pose, that will be enough
Cameras are clicking, lights of flashing
People will think you look quite dashing
Sit down in your limo, take a rest
Well, you could only do your best.

India Davies (9)
The Raleigh School

The Gym Poem

Time to start gym,
Make ourselves fit,
I really like it,
Cause I've got the kit.

The warm-up's too hard,
Breathtaking as well,
But I can do it,
Without any hell.

We're all left now,
For today and the next,
The teachers are kind,
But I've still got to flex.

The beam is too tricky,
But floor is my best,
Trampoline is fun,
But it's time for a rest.

It's the end for today,
I'm tired and drained,
But that will be the same,
Again and again!

Melissa Williams (9)
The Raleigh School

Autumn Is Here, Summer Has Gone

Autumn is here
Summer has gone
The trees are naked and bare
The leaves are twirling in the wind
And playing in the air

Autumn is here
Summer has gone
The leaves are not green anymore
But brown, red and gold

Autumn is at its end
But spring is here
Blossom sprouts
But best of all birds are singing
And playing in the air.

Andrew Wells (9)
The Raleigh School

Hallowe'en

H allowe'en, you can get lots of sweets
A ny time at Hallowe'en there's lot of people you can meet
L ike candy, love it so
L ike it a lot, go to www.Hallowe'en. co
O n the day we trick or treat
W e gather up all our sweets
E at them with a lick of the lips
E ven though we feel quite sick
N ight is brewing, time for sleep.

Katie Tame (9)
The Raleigh School

The Funniest Thing I Ever Saw

The funniest thing I ever saw was a parrot eating a burger
The funniest thing I ever saw was Michael Jackson with a blue nose
The funniest thing I ever saw was a man in a hamster suit
The funniest thing I ever saw was a clown dressed in an army suit
The funniest thing I ever saw was a pirate going shopping
The funniest thing I ever saw was nothing
The funniest thing I ever saw was a dinosaur drinking tea
The funniest thing I saw was nothing.

Jade Warr (8)
The Raleigh School

My Family

I like my brother Jake, he is *never* bad
He always cheers me up when I'm feeling sad

I have two naughty cats, they are very cheeky
When they come in the house they are very sneaky

I also like my dad, even when he's stressy
I think he gets angry because we're very messy

I really love my mum, she is very kind
I like her because she has a very good mind

And what about me - I'm a cheeky monkey
My mum always tells me I'm really rather hunky!

Harry Bennett (9)
The Raleigh School

The Show

I brushed her until she shone in the sun
I plaited her mane again and again
I put her saddle and bridle on
I also got the mud out of her hooves
I picked up my blue hat and put it on
There was my mum calling to see if we were ready
Down and down the road we went
I was nervous
She was too
There we were, me and my horse
Together.

Ellie Judd (10)
The Raleigh School

Football Madness

Football is my favourite sport
We're on a big, big court
What a shot, what a goal
That makes the score eleven-all
How many goals can I score
With the ball travelling along the floor?
I've got the ball, I'm going to shoot
Oh dear, it hit the wrong part of my boot
I can hardly bear to watch the ball
But what luck, I've scored a goal
At the end of the match, it is eleven-seven.

Oliver Hassard (9)
The Raleigh School

Winter

Dark days, still nights
Children having snowball fights.

Everything is standing still
The biting wind gives me a chill.

Snowflakes falling all around
The slippery ice on the ground.

The trees and bushes stand lost and bare
My breath is steamy in the freezing air.

The cold creeps underneath my skin
And makes me want to hurry in.

Huddled round the cosy fire
Hearing Christmas carols from the choir.

Warm radiators and water bottles in bed
Dreaming of summer holidays in my head.

Winter really isn't such a bad thing
And before you know it, here comes spring.

Hannah Hill (10)
The Raleigh School

My Cat

I have a black cat
She is rather fat
I love her to bits
And so that is that!

She can run like a cheetah
I bet you can't beat her
She is the best cat
And she couldn't be sweeter!

Her name is Blackie
And though she's a fatty
She simply rules
And she's always happy!

Victoria Holloway (10)
The Raleigh School

Young Writers - A Pocketful Of Rhyme Poems From Surrey

Poaching

P oaching is such a dreadful thing, why do people like poaching?
O n and on poaching goes, oh why do people like poaching?
A lways will be misery for animals, why do people like poaching?
C olchester rifles are used for poaching, oh why do people
  like poaching?
H undreds of people are poachers, but why do people like poaching?
I ll animals often die from poaching, why do people like poaching?
N othing is gained from poaching, so why do people like poaching?
G reat many poach, but why do people like poaching?

Oliver Hind (9)
The Raleigh School

I'm Nearly There

I'm getting ready for my race,
In the lines of two.
The man's about to blow the whistle:
Peep! Here we go.
Everyone is sprinting at the start,
Now I'm going into my jogging pace
I'm already out of breath.

Running, running, faster and faster,
There's two lions behind me, remember.
My heart is pounding,
I can't take it much longer.
Round the corner,
Here I come.

Sprinting, sprinting, faster and faster,
Mum and Rachel are shouting their heads off.
I'm nearly there, I'm nearly there,
'Come on, come on.'

Through the finish line, I'm getting my card
I've done it, I'm worn out.
Mum's there at the finish,
Waiting to give me a big hug.

Emily Runton (10)
The Raleigh School

The Seasons

This is all about the seasons and Christmas too,
And when in the summer, the sky is bright, bright blue
And in the winter the trees are like skeletons
And in the spring, trees are covered with pink blossom.

There is in autumn a crusty carpet of leaves,
Brown on the ground as you sit sipping a hot cup of tea,
It starts to get dark earlier and earlier
And you start to shiver, as you feel the coldness in the air.

There is in winter, lots of presents and snow,
You should feel the coldness when you reach down low,
The water is frozen, crumbling ice
And the trees look all gloomy, all bare and icy.

There is in spring lots of flowers and sun,
You enjoy the countryside as you do a long, long run,
You enjoy the yellow daffodils and the bluebells too,
The trees are covered in blossom as you run through.

There is in summer, sunshine and lots of sand
And on the beach everyone can hear the music being played
                                        by the band,
The sun shines bright and everybody is happy
And you watch the children playing frisbee, as you take your dog
                                        for a walk.

That was all about the seasons and Christmas too
And when in the summer, the sky is bright, bright blue
And in the winter, the trees are like skeletons
And in the spring, trees are covered in pink blossom.

Charlotte Piears (10)
The Raleigh School

The Boring Life Of A Cone

My life is boring, I wait and wait
Until I am needed somewhere like on a road
And I am reunited with my fellow cones
I hate it, I hate my life!

My life is boring, I get taken for granted
Everyone just knocks me over and kicks me around
I hate it, I hate my life!

My life is boring, all I get to do is wait and wait,
On the road it sucks, I am the one that makes the traffic flow
I make the trouble go,
I hate it, I hate my life!

My life is boring, I have to wake up early
And don't even get fed
I don't even know what food tastes like
I hate it, I hate my life!

My life is boring, all the other cones laugh at me
Because I actually have to work for a living
I hate it, I hate my life!

My life is boring, I got separated from my parents when I was ten
And I have not seen them since
I hate it, I hate my life!

My life is just so boring and so miserable
I really hate it, I really, really, really hate my life!

Samuel Gilbert (10)
The Raleigh School

Autumn Days

Autumn days are so beautiful
Golden leaves upon the trees
That fall onto the ground
And the last buzzing of the bees

Autumn days are full of life
Many birds are migrating
The squirrels, red and grey, are burying nuts
And hedgehogs are almost hibernating

Autumn days have something special
Called Bonfire Night
The bonfire is so big and warm
And the fireworks are so bright

Autumn days have tasty treats
Picking blackberries every day
Roasted chestnuts and apple pie
Having fun in a different way

Autumn days are wonderful
The last of the crystal blue skies
The trees with leaves of many colours
When you get out and enjoy the countryside.

Ellie Whitlock (10)
The Raleigh School

Noodle The Poodle

My dog is called Noodle
He's a funny looking French poodle
We called him Noodle because he always eats noodles
We thought it was an odd habit, so we researched it on Google
We found nothing, so we phoned the doctor, Floodle
He suggested to feed him biscuits, called Oodle Doodles
And now he's the happiest dog ever.

Callum Nixon (10)
The Raleigh School

The Throat Strangler

It slowly creeps through the forest's ferny floor, ready to strike
Strangling its prey tightly, round and round.

It has no legs, it has no arms,
But its muscles are as strong as Hercules!
They can grow up to the length of a double-decker bus
Just think how long that would be!

In zoos, in the wild these creatures are deadly
If you get too close, they'll get too feisty
Beware they're very vicious!

Their little throats may look small,
But they can swallow a whole female deer!
Be very, very careful . . .
Munch!

Holly Stroud (10)
The Raleigh School

Summer Poem

Colourful butterflies fly around in the sparkling blue sky
While I hear bumblebees buzz from flower to flower.

I watch fresh green grass as it sways in the breeze
And beautiful flowers all different bright colours.

The glistening sun shines on the calm swishing sea
Snow-white seagulls glide around while you're having a picnic
on the hot beach.

That magnificent blue sky starts to fade away
And the stars come out and shine all night.

Olivia Ellis (10)
The Raleigh School

Autumn

The long summer has gone and autumn is here,
There is lots of fun to be had at this time of year.

Stomping around in the crisp golden-brown leaves,
Which have gently fallen from the enormous bare trees.

The sound of *whizzing* fireworks, which light up the dark sky
The smell of smoking bonfires, which warm you as you stroll by.

Surely, everyone must love this time of year,
As the long summer has gone and now autumn is here!

Christie Dowling (10)
The Raleigh School

Summer Poem

Summer green is delightful
The shimmering sun shines like nothing else
Puffy clouds are in the bright skies of the Earth
Whilst caterpillars transform into butterflies
Dragonflies hang around the glittery pond
Big grey herons swoop fish out of the blue crystal waters
Pond-skaters skate the sparkling green water
And people's eyes shimmer like crystals in the sun
People wearing brightly coloured clothes
All the poppies and sunflowers have sprung out
Trees grow, whilst weeds slowly die.

Matt Gould (10)
The Raleigh School

My Family

My brother he is noisy
He is chatting all the time
And right now while he's talking
I'm making up this rhyme.

My sister she is crazy
It's really plain to see
And if you took a look at her
You wouldn't want to be me.

My pet, Star, she pees everywhere
Tabby's not as bad
Foster's always outside
And Blue just goes right mad.

My mum she is caring
My dad is just the same
We are one big happy family
Our life is a big fun game.

Eleanor Johnston (10)
The Raleigh School

When I Go Out . . .

When I go out on a summer's day it's surely very nice
When I go out on a winter's day it's surely not nice at all
When I go out on an autumn day the leaves are always falling
When I go out on a spring day it's the best day to be out at all!

Ellie Feary (8)
The Raleigh School

Sun

Bright, beaming, powerful source of light
Blinding anyone who dares look up
Gleaming on the bright world
Made from the sun's lovely yellow rays
Up, up in the sky
Looking all around
Its bright burning ball will burn you if you get too close
Its round face as yellow as a sunflower
As it scorches around the world
Leave it as it is until late dawn
Until night has come.

Isobel Marsh (7)
The Raleigh School

The Rocking Rainforest

Monkeys rushing from tree to tree
Flowing through the canopy
Frogs leaping from hot to cold
Vanilla so sticky, black and yellow
Gold lions roaring as loud as they can get
Giant snakes hissing around
With scales like a rough type of tree
Colourful parrots, frizzing like a rustling noise
Bubbling bubbles in the white clean water
This is what it's like to rock in the rainforest.

Jessica Caulder (9)
The Raleigh School

Great Green Gardens

Creaking swing seats, old and rusty
Scarlet roses, scent so sweet
Beautiful, dainty, pink petals
Brown and orange-coloured leaves
Floating around in the wind.

Brown bulrushes swaying in the breeze
Olive-coloured frogs leaping everywhere
Golden fish swimming in the pond
Water glittering in the sun
Pond-skaters dancing through the weeds.

Green, green grapevines
Soon to be ripe
Lush green grass blowing in the wind
Tomatoes turning from green to red
This is my garden.

Claire Robinson (9)
The Raleigh School

The Rainforest

Cold water bubbling roughly in the wind
Monkeys jumping quickly in the soft gentle breeze
Vines creeping slowly up enormous tropical trees
Spiders quickly climbing hot, misty, steamy leaves
Giant black-headed eagle, swooping down to catch its meal
And vanilla trees, as sticky as can be.

Jessica De Carvalho (9)
The Raleigh School

My Toddler Twins

They both like reading books and watching TV
And 'Stuart Little' is their favourite DVD.
Alicia loves princesses and all pretty flowers,
While Rex likes Batman who has super powers.
Alicia likes to dance, all over the place
And when Rex sees a football, round the garden he will race.
Alicia likes party skirts and wearing anything pink,
But Rex's favourite is a 'fire engine top', I think.
Alicia likes putting all my shoes on her feet
And we haven't found any food that Rex will not eat.
Rex likes cars and motorbikes and anything blue,
We have not yet found a puzzle that he cannot do.
Rex likes to read his Dumbo book almost every day,
While with make-up and lipstick, Alicia will always play.
Alicia thinks she's Cinderella and loves any sparkly jewel,
Now every Tuesday and Thursday they go to nursery school.
They both like watching Cbeebies and the Teletubbies
And play together all the time because they're special buddies.
They've grown so much and never rest,
But my toddler twins are still *the best!*

Verity Barnes (11)
The Raleigh School

My Magic Box

(Based on 'Magic Box' by Kit Wright)

I will put in my box . . .
The soft fluffy feel of Fluffer
The silky smoothness of my guinea pig's ear.

I will put in my box . . .
Mollie sitting on my lap with Auntie Clare reading to me
The taste of yummy chocolate mousse, the lady made
The first time me and my best friend made friends.

I will put in my box . . .
The collection of Amelia-Jane
The feel of my nanny's soft hand
My kind and fantastic teacher.

I will put in my box . . .
The smell of 'Red Woman'
The smell of my mother's lovely clothes
The hair of Izzy.

I will put in my box . . .
The kind helpful Chinese dragon
The helpful sister I have
The assistant called Mrs Strauss.

My box is made of gold and silver, studded with jewels.

Alice Thacker (8)
The Raleigh School

The Creature

My thick fur is as dark as night
My eyes are like the morning bright
I have four feet which move, one by one
I weigh an absolute ton
But I'm kind and gentle and have a ticklish tummy
In the jungle I look kind of funny.
I like to bathe in the mud and get smelly
I eat lots of food and fill up my belly
Tree climbing and sleeping are my favourite things
I dream of flying but don't have wings
Are you wondering by now what creature I am?
A bear-cat that's me and my name is Sam.

Ben Lock (10)
The Raleigh School

My Mum

My mum's a pharmacist
She goes a long way to get to work
My mum drives a silver VW Touran
My mum makes the best spaghetti
My mum supports Leicester.

My mum says I should go to more clubs
So I should get more muscly
My mum *has* to go to Sainsbury's every week
And spends loads of money
My mum has to get changed if she spills stuff down her T-shirt
And that's just my mum.

William Stanford (9)
The Raleigh School

My Cousin Scott

My cousin Scott is a cartoon drawer
He can draw anything in the world
If you ask for a dog, out comes a dog
Just like a drawing machine.

My cousin Scott is a tea lover
He is always up for a cup
You only need to mention the word 'tea'
And he says I'll have a cup.

My cousin Scott is a speedy eater
He always finishes first
Except if he's racing a dog of course
A dog just eats it up.

Christopher Bennett (8)
The Raleigh School

My Mother

My mother is the best
Better than all the rest
Because she has long hair
Her hair shines like the sunshine.

My mum treats me like a baby
She says, 'Of course sweetheart,' in a very loud way
She embarrasses me when I dance in the mirror
To my music or plays
She is embarrassing when she sings.

My mother is the best
And I love her.

Millie Franks (9)
The Raleigh School

The Aliens Are Invading Earth

The aliens are invading Earth
Oh look, they've gone through the turf
They've gone through every town
All I've got left is my dressing gown.

The aliens are invading Earth
Now I've got to cancel my surf
The aliens are all green
Oh look, one's called Dean.

Dominic Rawlins (8)
The Raleigh School

My Dad

My dad is a great dad
He can keep secrets
Play football
And break his arm.

He ran the 2001 marathon
When he took the shower out
He got a hammer on his hand.

My dad is a great dad
He has a Scotland hat that goes everywhere
He has eyes that never miss a Liverpool match
My dad hit a football at my face
Red card!

My dad
I love my dad.

Stuart McCully (8)
The Raleigh School

Animal's World

Vicious black and white tigers silently stalking prey
Lazy lions majestically snoozing
Deadly, humid, hot weather
Beautiful shiny fish glinting against the water
Dangerous piranhas snapping at other fish
Shiny, sparkling leaves dripping water to the ground
Itsy-bitsy small insects quickly scuttling along the jungle floor.

Joseph Nicholson (9)
The Raleigh School

All Alone

I was dreading the day when it came
I bet you can't imagine the pain
I was walking down the lane
When he grabbed me!

He demanded my money for lunch
And then he gave me a punch
I walked away and something went crunch
It was his Coke can!

When I went out to play
He told me to go away
It was a dreadful day
I felt like a needle in a haystack.

I went to the teacher right away
Because he said he would punch me the very next day
The teacher caught him at play
And now I'm as free as a bird!

Emma Tallick (10)
The Raleigh School

The Magic Box

(Based on 'Magic Box' by Kit Wright)

I will put in my box . . .
The scent of a beautiful red rose
The smell of burning firewood
The feel of a colourful rainbow.

I will put in my box . . .
The sound of lightning crashing to the ground
The taste of my favourite food
The magic of a wizard's spell.

I will put in the box . . .
The magic of old merry Santa
The golden magical moon
A piece of fairy dust.

I will put in my box . . .
The smell of ruby-red fire.
My box is made of silver and gold silk weaved by fairies.

Megan Richards (7)
The Raleigh School

My Dog Lucy

I love my dog called Lucy
I think she is a bit loopy
My dog is quite funny
We walk her when it's sunny
She barks at cats
My dad taught her that
I love my dog called Lucy.

Imogen Harms (7)
The Raleigh School

The Magic Box

(Based on 'Magic Box' by Kit Wright)

I will put in the box . . .
The smell of sweet yummy ice cream
The smell of burning toast
The smell of my friend's cute doggy.

I will put in the box . . .
The touch of my fluffy teddy
The touch of a fox's swishy tail
I can see a multicoloured rainbow
I can see a bright pointy star.

I will put in my box . . .
The sound of the magical sea
The sound of monkeys squealing.

My box is made of thick china
With gold pictures around
Inside it is gold.

Kay Bainbridge (7)
The Raleigh School

The Magic Box

(Based on 'Magic' Box' by Kit Wright)

I will put in the box . . .
The taste of glorious food.

I will put in my box . . .
The feeling of the sea and the smell of the air.

I will put in the box . . .
The sound of crabs clicking their pincers.

My magic box is made of the ancient underwater world.

Marcus Hutchings (7)
The Raleigh School

A Live, Spooky, Scary, Dark Rainforest

In a live, spooky, scary, dark rainforest
The weather is too humid and burning
Waving blue water running around
Green vines creeping up around
Dark brown trunks shooting to the light
Dark green tree bushes waving in a sudden wind
That blows to and fro
Silky slithering leaves slowly dripping water
Colourful creepy-crawlies sneaking underground
Black and orange tigers, lazily lying in a beaming, humid, sticky sun
Long, sneaky snakes wrapping around dark brown tree trunks
Loud, leaping frogs hopping from one lilypad to another lilypad
Silky, golden lions roaring at lazy tigers
Light brown monkeys swaying from one branch to another branch
Bright parrots gliding just above tree bushes.

Eleanor Chard (9)
The Raleigh School

The Beautiful Rock Garden

Listen to the water as it slops over the edge, *patter, patter, patter*
As it goes over the ledge, *patter, patter, patter*
Twisting, turning, bubbling
Lilypads the size of party plates
Stones as big as cannonballs
Crystal-clear water so cool to touch
Pretty flowers, an assortment of colours,
Yellow, purple, reds and oranges
The smell of flowers and rain - sweet and pure
Tall, commanding trees will stretch out their branches
As if to protect the rock garden.

Angus Cook (9)
The Raleigh School

The Jungle

Brown monkeys swinging tree to tree
Scarlet parrots glide through the blue sky
Green creepers twisting up the whistling trees
Brown leaves crackling as they hit the jungle floor.

Lemurs look for fresh green leaves on the treetops
And the fresh blue water in the stream
Rushing down the jungle
Tigers looking for their prey
As the snakes slither through the green trees
Black-spotted cheetahs running in the golden, orange sun
With dark brown trunks growing higher and higher.

The banana tree has the lovely yellow bananas
With the massive banana leaves
The rain on the leaves is like crystals
The jungle is always awake, day and night
Alive with the brilliant sounds and colours of the beautiful jungle life
This is the amazing jungle.

Edward Barber (9)
The Raleigh School

Rainforest Rock

Rocking rainforest, rocking rainforest
Whipping rains, olive greens, tangling vines
Fast dripping drops of all different kinds
Greens, golds, yellows too
These are the leaves, the leaves
Of the jungle breeze . . .
Hummingbirds sipping nectar
Hum, hum, hum
Humid, damp, the jungle now
Rocking rainforest, rocking, just rocking.

Alice Richardson (9)
The Raleigh School

School Dinners

I hate school dinners, they're disgusting, absolutely vile
Just walking into the hall makes me sick
Then there's the older kids, getting up from the table and breathing
School dinnery breath all over you.

I look down at my plate, it's the same again
Mouldy cabbage, dry spinach,
Boiled Brussels sprouts and mushy peas
Yuck!

The puddings are worse, watery rice pudding
Lumpy custard that tastes like glue
Overcooked treacle sponge and soggy banana cake
Ugh!
I hate school dinners!

Ben Thompson (10)
The Raleigh School

Below The Canopy

Hurried monkeys devouring
Dripping honeycombs on dark trunks
As creepers shake the vanilla tree
The shimmer of light showing the intense snake
In the dense fields of scarlet and golden leaves.

Looking up at the sky is a vivid hood of shaking leaves
Their veins glinting in the golden sun
Water like jewels on their patterned surface
Vines overwhelming the clarity of trees reaching the light
Above the canopy tall, cocoa beans dropping into the soggy
undergrowth deep.

Oliver Harry (10)
The Raleigh School

The Magic Box
(Based on 'Magic Box' by Kit Wright)

I will put in the box . . .
The soul of water
The sound of last words
The feel of smooth skin.

I will put in the box . . .
Smooth air
The sound of crunching crisps
The loveliness.

I will put in the box . . .
The sound of footsteps
A smell of smoke
The sight of trees.

I will put in the box . . .
A taste of pizza.

My box is made of
The core of the world.

Joshua Henderson (7)
The Raleigh School

Midnight In The Rainforest

Midnight in the rainforest
Is a very special time
A time for animals from far and wide
To gather in a clearing
Yeah, it's party time
Everyone turns up
No one's ever late
For the big surprise that awaits
So midnight in the rainforest
It's a very special time.

Katie Thacker (9)
The Raleigh School

I Went Around The World One Day

I went around the world one day
I saw a shark, hip hip hooray
I saw dolphins and tortoises too
I nearly stepped in camel poo
I went to Germany, I went to France
A magician put me in a trance
I went on planes, I went in cars
I went in a rocket to see the stars
I bought new books, I bought new toys
I bought new clothes and found new joys
I went around the world one day
I'm really glad I went away.

Oliver Beney (10)
The Raleigh School

My Big, Black, Cuddly Dog

My dog's big, black and cuddly
He's extremely cute
He's always being a lunatic
He's always stealing my boots
He's furry like a teddy bear
He's always barking mad
He likes a tickle on his chin
It's the best he's ever had
He likes to go for a run round a huge park
And when the postman's at the door
He sometimes gives a bark
My dog is very funny, I love him very much
Thank You Lord for making dogs
Thank You very much!

James Smith (10)
The Raleigh School

An Autumn Day

I wake up early on a beautiful autumn day
I run downstairs to see the flowers play
I listen to the birds singing, sweet tunes
I faintly remember yesterdays at Junes
I watch the cars drive by, the people walking in the woods
I wonder if my day will be as best as it could
I smell the moist grass, blowing in the wind
I see the plants trying to get free, but they can't because
they are pinned

I go outside to feel the fresh air
I hear the sound of a busy road, *beep,* that I cannot bear
I watch the apples growing on the tree
I look at the apples that have fallen, they be
I glance at the fallen leaves
I wonder how they get to be all different, beautiful colours,
some like bees
I realise how lucky I am to be here, in such a wonderful time,
in a wonderful place
Now that is the best autumn day!

Rebecca Fox (10)
The Raleigh School